roadSIGNS

Travel Tips for Authentic Living

Betty Healey

Published by Creative Bound International Inc.
on behalf of Conrod-Jacques Consultants Inc. www.peopleHEALTH.ca

ISBN 1-894439-11-2
Printed and bound in Canada

Design and production by **Creative Bound International Inc.**
www.creativebound.com 1-800-287-8610
Gail Baird, Managing Editor • Wendy O'Keefe, Creative Director

Cover design and coordinating illustrations by Tracy-Lynn Chisholm
Author photograph by Jacquie Milner

Printing number 10 9 8 7 6 5 4 3 2 1

National Library of Canada Cataloguing in Publication

Healey, Betty J., 1950-
        Roadsigns : travel tips for authentic living / Betty J. Healey.

Includes bibliographical references.
ISBN 1-894439-11-2

        1. Conduct of life. I. Title.

BF637.C5H42 2003   158   C2003-904446-7

Dedicated to My Life Partner ~ Jim
"Thank you for seeing the diamond within."

My Spirit Friends
Deedy and Linda
and
My Spirit Guide, Tanis

Contents

Why *road*SIGNS?

I have traveled many roads from gravel back roads to eight-lane highways during my lifetime. In search of our Canadian roots, my husband and I have even driven every kilometer of the Trans-Canada Highway from Cape Spear, Newfoundland, to Long Beach, British Columbia. On our many journeys we have explored cow paths, laneways and mountain passes throughout New England, the Midwest and west coast of the United States, Scotland, Scandinavia and numerous other locales.

On each of our journeys, we have encountered signs—signs that direct us, predict the road ahead, warn us of upcoming hazards, provide us with the speed limit, animal crossings, and so on. When in unfamiliar territory, we've learned to watch for the signs, knowing they will provide us with the information we need and guide us to our chosen destination. In everyday territory, however, signs are rarely seen; they are part of the all-too-familiar scenery.

And so it is with life: when our life takes a turn to the unfamiliar, we find ourselves paying attention, but when we are in our comfort zone, the signs go unnoticed.

My call to write this book began with signs. In the summer of 2000, we made a decision to purchase a property in rural Ontario, our need to escape city living finally taking top priority. For the first time in many years, I was faced with a new challenge—commuting. Two to three times each week, I would climb into my car, start the ignition, open the garage door, and with a silent prayer for a safe drive, begin the 100-kilometer trip to Montreal. In the early morning air, I would breathe deeply, absorbing my peaceful surroundings. Leaving the quiet beauty of rural Ontario, my drive would begin. After what seemed like a few short minutes, I would arrive at my destination in downtown Montreal.

Frequently I found myself pausing as I locked up the car for the day, asking myself, "How did I get here so quickly? What did I miss along the way?" The familiar route I traveled seemed to guide my car forward as I was lost somewhere in the passageways of my mind. The trip was usually just a blur of images. Driving, it seemed, was an altered state of consciousness. Disconnected from the experience, I was paying attention yet I wasn't. I would wonder, "Were there signs along the road that I should have paid attention to—and if so, what were they telling me?"

I did not get it at first. One day I simply had a great "aha" moment. Not only was I engaging the cruise control for my car, I recognized that I was, more often than not, doing the same thing with my life. I frequently did not see the signs, those important messages which the universe provides us everyday. I could not say for sure, but I felt that I was losing out on something really important, something that might affect and possibly change the course I was on.

And so the idea of *road*SIGNS was born. It was a call to attention—my call to begin to inhabit my life more fully. It also put me on notice to take my writing seriously and to share it with others. It began as a monthly e-mail newsletter and grew into this book.

I welcome you to *road*SIGNS, and invite you to join me in paying attention and being more present in your own life. It is a journey of taking responsibility for yourself and being open to the messages the universe offers you every day; a journey of reflection, understanding and learning; a journey of living a life of purpose, guided by your core values and a respect for Mother Earth. *road*SIGNS serve as our guideposts, the *road* referring to the journey of life, and the SIGNS, those Significant Insightful "Gold Nuggets" informing your Soul and Spirit.

There are no instructions for reading this book. It is written as a guide in the hope that each sign presented leads you to some personal insights. Use it intuitively. Turn to that section of the book that attracts you; read it in whatever way suits your needs. There is no specific order. Each chapter presents a SIGN and how this SIGN spoke to me. It may say something else to you. That is the intention. The chapters are brief, each one offering the lesson I drew as I reflected on the meaning of the SIGN that had captured my attention.

Each lesson is followed by a Travelogue, containing questions for journaling, and stories and exercises. Give yourself the time to reflect on the questions and to complete the exercises. These will lead you to greater clarity and pull you into living your life more fully. Questions themselves are also SIGNS. They do not always require an immediate answer; they may simply need to be held. As poet Rainer Maria Rilke suggests, we need to "love the questions themselves" and live our way into an answer.

Each chapter concludes with a Travel Tip, the coordinates for the map of your life. They are intended to highlight the key point of each chapter, as well as awaken you from your dream state—and alert you to the possibility that you may be drifting through your life. Travel Tips are summarized in the Epilogue.

As you read this book, I encourage you to start paying attention to the SIGNS in your life. This may take many forms—from actual road signs to a conversation you overheard which seemed to be meant for you, stories and metaphors that make you well up with emotion, a quote in a book which struck a chord, or something a friend shares with you that puts you on notice. They are the "aha" moments—those brain cramps, which throw your thinking off course for a few seconds and which signal "Pay Attention!"

The message may not always be obvious. You sense there is something calling to you. Be patient. Sometimes we listen without hearing; observe without seeing; touch without feeling. The SIGN is a signal to STOP and take time to be quiet. Allow yourself to leave the road you are currently on and pull off to the side. If you don't, you may miss something important.

Start taking notice of SIGNS. All of us have spent too many hours of too many days speeding through our lives, feeding our personalities while ignoring our souls. This is your invitation to wake up and enjoy the journey—your authentic life. The practice of paying attention may save your life; if nothing else, it will certainly make the ride more interesting.

As people grow old, they actually become more awake—they earn a new reality. Their consciousness is a magnificent bridge between that world and ours.
Lynn Andrews, *Tree of Dreams*

PART 1

Finding the Quiet Place Within

Road Liable to Subsidence

If you do not go within, you go without.
Neale Donald Walsch, *Conversations with God*

In the summer of 1999, my husband Jim and I traveled to Scotland. We had long heard the call to visit this country, perhaps our own Celtic roots reaching out for us. It was remarkable how much at home we felt there, as if the place had always been known to us. We found ourselves pinching one another and saying, "We're in Scotland!" just to remind ourselves we were not back home in Canada.

Many of the road signs in Scotland differed from those at home. On a back road somewhere on the Isle of Skye, where sheep were the only real traffic we had to deal with, we came upon a sign that read "Road Liable to

Subsidence." Having no idea what the sign meant, we took a photo and began to ruminate about what it was that we were supposed to be paying attention to.

This was our first awakening, that moment when both of us realized that perhaps *road*SIGNS had some deeper, more profound meaning. Upon returning home, I decided to check out the meaning of "subsidence." The definition, compliments of the Houghton Mifflin Canadian Dictionary, is as follows:

Subsidence n / subside v: to sink to a lower or normal level; to sink or settle down, as in a sofa; to sink to the bottom, settle, as in sediment; to become less agitated or active; abate.

"Settling down"—those words spoke to me. It is so easy to get on the treadmill of life and forget to take time for meditation, a walk outside, a cup of coffee with a friend or simply daydreaming at my desk. The world of work increasingly demands more of us. And this is matched by our busy lives beyond the walls of the organization—commitments to service organizations, sports with our children, housework, this and that. Time is literally chewed up, and none of it is set aside just for us.

Is it time to allow ourselves to be "liable to subsidence," to settle down or sink back into something, to break into the routine busyness of our lives? I frequently wonder, if I give all of myself away to the doings of everyday, what will be left for me? And, when there is nothing left, then what?

I know it is in the quiet moments that we can experience the truth of who we are. It is then that we can actually begin to see and hear the SIGNS, to reflect on them and ponder the greater meaning.

Travelogue

Journaling Questions
- How much time do you take each day to stop, breathe and be quiet —to settle down?
- Does this occur only when your head finally makes contact with the pillow at the end of the day?

The Doing/Being Continuum

This exercise is designed to help you gain some perspective on the degree of balance in your life. In his book *Simple Living in a Complex World*, David Irvine tells the story of an old yogi master who sat meditating all day under a tree in the center of a busy city. The businesspeople and street vendors criticized his lack of initiative, seeing him as a non-contributor to their way of life. Eventually, however, he simply became part of the scenery, his daily presence accepted by all except one young businessman. This man's anger at seeing the yogi "sleeping" under a tree reached such a pitch that one day, as he was rushing to work, he decided to confront the older man. "How can you sit here all day, every day, in a trance?" he shouted. The yogi slowly opened his eyes, raised his head so as to look at the young man directly, and said, "My son, you are the one who is in a trance."

We are left wondering who is truly in a trance—the yogi who spends his day meditating or the businessman who is caught up in the busyness of doing.

The answer, however, is that both of them are in their own type of trance. What we need in life is balance, an appropriate portion of both being and doing mixed into the recipe. We need to feed ourselves through achievement in the external world, and we need at times to subside, to take time to connect within, to nurture our spirit. Are you living an integrated life?

Try this:

1. Ask three people who know you very well to give you feedback. Ask where they would place you on the Doing/Being Continuum?

   Doing |__|__|__|__|__|__|__|__|__|__|__|__| Being

2. At the same time, complete this for yourself? Does your perception mirror the feedback you are receiving from others?
3. Make a note of three things you long to do and never have enough time for. If you did those things, which direction would you be moving on the continuum?
4. Briefly review your journey over the past few years. Where were you three years ago? Where would you like to be three years hence?
5. What commitment do you need to make, to yourself and others, to lead a more integrated life?
6. Now what?

Travel Tip

Along most major highways, we see signs posted for REST AREA, an opportunity to pull out of the traffic, get out of the car, take care of our biological needs and stretch those cramped legs. When we are caught up in the busyness of our day-to-day routine, involving work and numerous other "doings," we also need to stop and rest; we need time to work out the spiritual cramps, the accumulation of doing in lieu of being. Make a commitment to begin scheduling a minimum of 10 minutes each day to subside—your time for reflection, quiet and breathing. This may be the most important 10 minutes of every day.

Am I Giving My Power Away?

Our deepest fear is not that we are inadequate.
Our deepest fear is that we are powerful beyond measure.
It is our Light, not our Darkness, that most frightens us.

We ask ourselves, who am I to be brilliant, gorgeous, talented,
fabulous? Actually, who are you NOT to be?
Marianne Williamson, *Return to Love*

Have you ever found yourself in a situation where you felt compelled to "give in," knowing that what you were being asked to do was not in your best interest? Life presents most of us with this kind of challenge almost every day, those occasions where we believe we must compromise or say "yes" when we really want to say "no." Our daily routine is filled with a series of YIELD signs, a merging of ourselves into the mainstream of work and society. Whenever I see this sign, it causes me to examine where in my life I am not not being true to myself; where in my life am I giving my power away?

If I really want to inhabit my days with purpose, I need ask myself when it is that I have a sense of being out of integrity with myself. What parts of me am I failing to acknowledge as I yield to the expectations of others—clients, friends or family? Am I being authentic—true to myself?

It has been my experience that I am often too willing to put myself on the back burner. Perhaps it is that I do not value my own strengths and gifts enough or that I simply believe that what others have to offer, their knowledge or expertise, is greater or better than mine. The result has been that I lose my sense of personal power. I fail to see the brilliance of my own light shining. I am too focused on bowing before the light of others.

As you look around your everyday environment, whether at home or at work, you may wish to begin to check in with yourself and study how you respond to different situations. Are you generally the person others will come to because they know you will say yes? Remember the old commercial, "Give it to Mikey, he'll eat it." Is it now, "Give it to _____, she'll/he'll do it"? In what circumstances do you want to say "no," but give in anyway? I am not suggesting that "YES" is something we must avoid, however we need to begin to discern when saying "yes" is in our best interest—and when it is not.

We also need to assess the choices we make everyday that allow us to feel purposeful, and the work opportunities that build our sense of personal mastery, allowing us to employ our skills, knowledge and strengths. Organizations are notorious for wanting to generalize the skill level of individuals versus building on unique differences. We are asked to do things that are not in our area of expertise or of particular interest to us. These things simply de-energize us.

Life is a test. Your boss wants you to hand over your power to him or her, demanding long hours, accompanied by unreasonable work expectations. A family member or friend wants to engage you in a gossip exchange, and while you know gossip is emotional sabotage, you yield. Your teenage son pushes and pushes to get his own way, sometimes playing the game of pitting you against your spouse. You finally give in, even though you feel the decision is wrong. You begin to notice that empty, knawing feeling in the pit of your stomach, a sure indication that you are not staying plugged into your own power. It's time to check in with yourself and your own Yield Barometer.

Travelogue

Questions for Reflection

- What part of myself am I yielding—giving up, surrendering or letting go of—that defines who I am as a person?
- What do I need to start saying "no" to?
- What steps am I prepared to take to achieve this?

Disconnected From Your Battery

Living in rural Ontario requires having a reliable vehicle. Never before have four wheels been as important to me. Often I am arriving home late, after meeting with a client in either Ottawa or Montreal. Driving through Alexandria, the car more often than not automatically arrives in the parking lot of the local grocery store in search of last-minute ingredients for a simple meal. When my car—my road warrior, Maxie—began to sputter and spit last fall, I became concerned, but deciding the symptoms were not serious, I delayed going to the garage. Then, homeward bound one night, she wouldn't start— a load of fresh ingredients in the car and already late. I said a silent prayer. She started on the third try. I patted the steering wheel with a silent "thank you." Off we went home.

The next morning, another busy day filled with appointments and things to do, I returned to the driver's seat. Turned the key. No response. Jim poked his nose out the door, listening for any sign of life in the engine. Shaking his head, he returned inside to call the CAA. The mechanic arrived after what seemed to be too long a wait, fueling my impatience. He opened the hood and emerged smiling. "Nothing serious, your cables were simply disconnected from your battery," he informed me.

Maxie was disconnected from her battery. And then the "aha" moment: my fatigue and impatience indicated that I, too, was disconnected from my battery. I was ignoring that empty feeling inside me again, working on a contract that took me into Montreal three days out of five, yielding to the demands of this schedule, the client, and the rigors of commuting. I was disconnected from my battery, drifting further and further from my sense of power, the result of focusing on everyone and everything but myself.

Here's a challenge. Write your story, "Disconnected from My Battery." Just write it. Don't question it; let it pour out from your soul. No grammar concerns or editing; let the words flow onto the paper and see what happens.

- Where does this story begin and end?
- When are you disconnected from your battery?
- What is your learning from your story?

Travel Tip

It's time for a tune-up, time to check your battery, your oil and your fuel gauge to ensure that you are both connected to your battery *and* running on a full tank. Like our vehicle, we need to check in with our power source.

Occasionally we must yield as we merge into the busyness of life, but if all we do is yield, we will become lost in the traffic. Knowing when to yield (and when not to) is important. On our journey of life, a connection to our personal battery, that deep sense of who we are and how we want to be of service, is what will help us go the distance.

A Radical Sabbatical

We nourish the soul when we find value in the stillness of the moment,
recognizing that the present time is the only time there is.
Gerald Jampolsky

A few years ago I was drawn to an article in *Fast Company* entitled "Radical Sabbaticals." The article featured a number of young professionals who had been in the fast lane and who, after working hard and fast for a number of years, decided to take four to six months off to catch their breath, travel or learn something new; to renew and to get back in touch with themselves.

Ah, the younger generation, I thought, they really know how to live. So many members of my generation are "doing addicts." Renewal—getting back in touch with ourselves—is a retirement project. But the idea of a radical sabbatical had taken hold. "Why *can't* I stop?" I wondered. Is it time, at the age of almost 50? Perhaps this younger generation knows something about living that I do not.

While the idea of a radical sabbatical had registered with me, I had difficulty giving myself permission to actually do it. Like many of us, I found myself barreling through life, running the stop signs, completely caught up in my busy schedule. The idea of coming to a full stop terrified me; although I knew how to be quiet for brief periods of time, I did not really understand the practice of "being." A radical sabbatical would take me to that place.

Then life intervened. Like the double STOP sign located not far from our home, I received two wake-up calls. The first stop sign came early in 2001, when I was faced with a major decision regarding my consulting business.

I had founded my consulting practice in 1997, and had considered stepping away from it on many occasions. After leaving a 25-year career in health care, I found myself immediately engaged in consulting projects, a continuation of much of the work I was doing at St. Mary's Hospital. I did not give myself the time necessary to fully evaluate what I wanted the nature of my work to be and what values would serve to guide me. The absence of clarity resulted in a lack of focus—doing a little of this and a little of that. The time came, however, when I absolutely knew that I needed time to reflect, to understand and to redirect. And yet there was always work to be done—marketing, planning or delivering workshops.

In August of 2000, I accepted a full-time contract with one of my clients. It offered the security of a continuous income, something that seemed to be important after buying our new country home. I thought it would take the pressure off for awhile, but what I found was the opposite. Instead of being able to breathe easier, I began to feel as if I was suffocating. I had lost the independence I had gained as an external consultant. I needed to commute to Montreal three to four days each week. I continued to serve a number of other clients— but not well. I found myself *doing* more and *being* less. Here I was in this rural Ontario paradise with no time to enjoy it. By early 2001, I felt increasingly disconnected from me and the reason I had started *people*HEALTH in the first place. This was my first STOP sign, but I continued to ignore it, telling myself I needed to work and that I had made a commitment to my client.

Then in June of 2001, my mother-in-law began a series of tests. I volunteered to go with her to doctor's appointments to help translate the medical jargon. It was a privilege for me, as my mom-in-law is a very special lady. When the CT scan results came back, we were shocked—probable ovarian cancer, a devastating possibility. This was my second STOP sign. A desire to be available for her and my family was the permission slip I needed. I ended my contract. I knew my work was done, I was simply lingering. I was free at last.

This was the beginning of my "radical sabbatical" and a new way of living. The voices in my head and heart demanded to be heard. It was time to remember and to respond to the questions: "Why are you here?" and "How are you to serve?"

Do you hear the same voices? What would it take for you to come to a full stop, to begin a radical sabbatical? Where in your life are you seeing the "double STOP sign"? What recent wake-up calls are whispering in your heart, waiting to be heard?

I know it feels scary to stop! For the first time in 30 years, I found myself not working. With more emphasis on the *being* than *doing*, I realized I did not know how to BE. I was a "doing addict." I believe most of us are, as we hurdle through life, failing to see—or ignoring—the SIGNS warning us to stop.

Since beginning my sabbatical, I have learned a very important lesson: that throughout my lifetime I have valued myself more for what I do—my work and the roles that I play—than who I am. Without a job to go to, a client to serve or a proposal to prepare, I had difficulty seeing who I was or what difference I was making to the world. Yet I profoundly understood that stopping was not only necessary, it would be the source of my survival, an opportunity to reconnect with myself and to understand my higher purpose.

I recognize that not everyone can indulge in a "radical sabbatical" as I have, but we *can* create the space in our life to be quiet and to reconnect with ourselves. Those quiet places are the think-tanks for our souls. Are you ready for the challenge?

Travelogue

Journaling Questions

- What life experiences have been real wake-up calls for you, your STOP signs?
- Write about one of your STOP signs and consider the following:
  How did you respond to it?
  What did you learn from it?
  How did it change your life?

What the Heart Knows

Dr. Mehmet Oz, director of the Cardiovascular Institute at Columbia Presbyterian Center, believes that our heart is a formidable teacher. He reminds us that the heart nourishes our body, pumping oxygen and nutrients out through a network of arteries reaching all other areas of the body. It recycles deoxygenated blood to the lungs, so it can be purified and ready for distribution elsewhere. We would not survive without our heart. But the heart knows something that we as human beings do not seem to understand. The first thing the heart does is nourish itself. The cardiac arteries, which feed the muscle that keeps the heart pumping strongly, are the first arteries to come off the aorta. The heart knows that unless it is strong, that unless it feeds itself first, it will not serve the rest of the body well.

What can we learn from the heart? If we do not keep ourselves strong, take time to nourish our spirit and care for ourselves, we will not be able to serve the other important people in our lives. The story of the heart reminds us of the importance of stopping and reconnecting with our own sense of purpose, of honoring ourselves and the gifts we bring to our world. As Derek Walcott expressed in his poem "Sea Grapes," "the time will come when, with elation you will greet yourself arriving at your own door, in your own mirror, and each will smile at each other's welcome, and say, sit here. Eat. You will again love the stranger who was yourself."

Travel Tip

Take time to STOP, pause, breathe and reflect. When something calls to you, like a child tugging at your sleeve, do not dismiss it. Allow yourself to leave the road you are currently on. Pull off on a side road or simply stop on the shoulder. You may miss something important if you fail to take the time to consider the SIGNS or the questions in your life and the message they contain. Stopping may result in a change in your life, a link to something from the past, or a lesson to be learned. STOP means STOP!

Children Being Children

My goal is to say or do one outrageous thing every week.
Maggie Kuhn, founder of the Grey Panthers

I love this sign. It is posted in many of the small communities locally. It reminds me that I was a child once, and makes me wonder where this child is —and the childlike wonder that came with her. Children see the world differently than we do. I want to reclaim some of the happiness and freedom I knew back then, and I ask myself:

- What do children see that I no longer see?
- What do they experience in life that I have lost sight of?

- Am I still able to relate to the world with childlike wonder or have I become too tarnished?
- What can I learn from children that I need to remember?

This is what came to me:

When I look at a patch of dandelions, I see a
bunch of weeds that are taking over my yard.

Children see flowers for Mom and blowing white fluff you can wish on.

When I look at an old drunk and he smiles at me,
I see a smelly, dirty person who probably wants money.

Children see someone smiling at them and they smile back.

When I hear music I love, I know I can't carry a tune
and don't have much rhythm so I sit self-consciously and listen.

Children feel the beat and move to it. They sing out the words.
If they don't know them, they make up their own.

When I feel wind on my face, I brace myself against it.
I feel it messing up my hair and pushing me back as I walk.

Children close their eyes, spread their arms and fly with it,
until they fall to the ground laughing.

When the leaves begin to fall from the trees, I prepare
myself for hours of raking and cleaning up the gardens.

Children see piles of leaves to jump into, covering themselves
and basking in the earthy smells of a warm fall day.

When I pray, I say thee and thou and grant me this, give me that.

Children say, "Hi God! Thanks for my toys and my friends. Please keep the bad dreams away tonight. Sorry, I don't want to go to Heaven yet. I would miss my Mommy and Daddy."

When I see a mud puddle I step around it.

I see muddy shoes, tracks on the floor and dirty carpets.

Children jump in it. They see dams to build,
rivers to cross, and worms to play with.

When I see snow falling, I think of the roads and difficult driving conditions and a driveway to shovel.

Children see potential—forts and snow people. They see the many sizes, shapes and patterns within the individual snowflakes.

When someone asks me to draw, I tense up. I am not an artist! I stare at the paper and hesitate to apply color, to sketch, to draw anything for fear it won't be good enough.

Children race to the paper, crayons and paint brushes, never doubting the artist that lurks inside. They begin to draw with reckless abandon.

Do you find yourself craving for the child within you to reappear? What were the toys or games that entertained you for hours? What was it you wanted to do when you grew up? What is your child trying to tell you, asking you to remember? What are the children in your life trying to teach you?

If we allow them to, children can teach us more than we teach them. We need to find opportunities to reconnect with the children in our lives, as well as with our own inner child, to start watching our children at play and wonder what we are being asked to remember. Take the time to enjoy the little things in life a little more and to try to remember how your child saw things years ago. Today, take the time to sing and dance and laugh! Today, take time to play and to make angels in the snow, bury yourself in a pile of leaves, jump on a trampoline or go hurtling across the water on a rubber tube just for the sheer joy of the experience. I plan to.

Travelogue

Journaling Questions
- When was the last time you let your inner child out to play?
- What was it you wanted to do when you grew up?
- What were the toys or games that entertained you for hours?
- What is your inner child trying to tell you, asking you to remember?
- What are the children in your life trying to teach you?

Watch the Children
Take a moment and pause. Watch a child at play. Observe an infant when he or she laughs and gurgles. As you watch, can you feel the energy

shift inside you? Describe what this feels like. Draw it. (Yes, you are an artist. You just forgot!)

Share your drawing with a friend. Compare notes. Ask what your friend sees in the drawing that you do not. What do you hear/see each other yearning for? What would you like to start doing, again, that responds to the call of your inner child?

Travel Tip

Turn the car radio up loud and sing along, or better still, sing in the shower as you start your day. Play street hockey with the kids next door. Swap funny stories with a friend. Host a "Whine and Jeeze" party; let people get things off their chests and then have a good chuckle. Laughter, music and fun open our hearts and ease the difficulties we sometimes encounter on the journey. They lubricate our cylinders and give us better mileage. We all need to "lighten up" at times. It helps us live life enthusiastically.

PART 2

A Road Map for My Soul

The Big Rocks in My Life

"Values are the prisms through which all self-information passes,
and they are the filter through which all decisions are crystallized.
They can anchor you in place or move you to the ends of the earth."
Deborah P. Bloch & Lee J. Richmond, *SoulWork*

A few years ago, I attended a seminar where the instructor was giving a lecture on work-life balance, seeing the real priorities in our life. At a certain point is the lecture, he stopped speaking. Pausing, he reached under the table and pulled out a wide-mouth, gallon-sized jar. On a table next to the jar, he placed some fist-sized rocks. Then the quiz began.

"How many of these rocks do you think we can fit in the jar?" he asked.

Several of us guessed at a number and then he proceeded, "Let's find out." He set one rock in the jar, then another and another until the jar was full. Then he asked, "Is the jar full?" Everybody looked at the rocks and agreed that it was.

The instructor looked out at us, then reached under the table and retrieved a bucket of gravel. He dumped some of the gravel into the jar and shook it. The gravel settled into the smaller spaces left between the rocks.

He smiled and said again, "Is the jar full?" This time we hesitated, then responded, "Probably not."

"Good!" he replied, and he reached under the table and brought out a bucket of sand. He poured the sand into the jar; it filtered down into the spaces left by the rocks and the gravel.

Once more, the instructor asked us if the jar was full. This time we responded with a resounding "NO!" He then proceeded to grab a pitcher of water and pour the contents into the jar.

Finally he stopped and turned to us and asked, "So, what was the point of this exercise?" After a few guesses, he proceeded to explain, "The point is: If I had not put the big rocks in first, would they have been able to fit in the jar?"

I am sure many of you have heard a version of this story. I often use it myself during workshops to highlight the idea of putting the big rocks of our lives in place first. What are the big rocks? They are our core values, those principles that define who we are and which we do not want to compromise under any circumstances.

Having said this, you may find that you do not know what your big rocks are. I often ask coaching clients to tell me about their core values. The response is often a blank look, not because there is an absence of values, but because they have not taken the time previously to consider the question.

I use the following analogy, to help them get started:

Imagine that you are holding two balls of similar size—one made of rubber, one made of quartz crystal. If you drop these balls on a hard surface you will have different results. The rubber ball will bounce back, the crystal one will crack, perhaps even shatter.

The quartz ball represents those values which are so precious to you that you dare not drop them. Dropping them would mean that some aspect of you would shatter or crack. These are the BIG ROCKS, your core values, the values which define who you are and how you wish to live in the world.

The rubber ball when dropped, however, bounces back. It will not break; it is resilient. It represents those things in life that, while important to you, you can drop from time to time and retrieve later. They are the gravel and sand that can be sifted down into the jar once the big rocks have been set in place.

This chapter's *road*SIGN serves to remind us that we need to take the time to reflect on, understand and identify our core values. They are essential guideposts, prisms through which we can filter our choices.

I encourage you to not lose sight of your BIG ROCKS. Take the time to identify them. Examine how you live them, in the different parts of your life. Determine in what circumstances your choices are aligned with your core values and in what circumstances they are not. Re-examine them on a regular basis and reflect on their importance in defining who you are. Here is a quick checklist you can also use:

- What values define me as a person?
- Has anything changed recently that would indicate a need to revise my values?
- In the last seven days, how have I modeled my values to others, both at home and at work?
- What changes do I need to introduce into my life so that I can live my values more fully?

Living by our values allows us to live life "full out." As you reconnect with your values, you will find that they are essential to living an authentic life, to feeling whole.

Travelogue

Identifying My Big Rocks

The list of words that follow will help you to identify what values are important to you. It is an incomplete list, so feel free to add words that represent values you do not see listed there. Review the entire list, and then circle those values you believe to be most important to you. Now, narrow down the list. Record your top three to five values in the space provided on the next page.

Truth	Decisiveness	Honesty
Efficiency	Security	Originality
Initiative	Love	Duty
Environmentalism	Freedom	Prosperity
Power/Authority	Inspiring	Respect
Control	Competence	Fairness
Courage	Harmony	Order
Competition	Openness	Spirituality
Excitement	Secure Environment	Adventure
Creativity	Change/Variety	Collaboration
Happiness	Sincerity	Humor/Fun
Honour	Inner Peace	Tradition
Family	Status Quo	Gratitude
Obedience	Wisdom	Safety
Financial Security	Flexibility	Service
Community	Perspective	Patience
Integrity	Promise Keeping	Empathy/Understanding
Peace	Recognition	Forgiveness
Loyalty	Learning	Grace

Dependability	Justice	Independence
Trust	Quality	Hope
Excellence	Health	Support
Teamwork	Responsiveness	Balance
Intuition	Fulfillment	Innovation
Profitability	Sense of Purpose	Leadership
Mastery	Strength of Character	Achievement
Friendship	Self-control	Beauty
Influence	Authentic Living	Active Listening

What are your BIG ROCKS, your core values?

_____

_____

_____

_____

_____

Journaling Questions

• How frequently do you check in with your values and evaluate the extent to which you are living them?

- What commitment would you need to make today to live your values more fully?
- Are you ready to commit? What does this mean?

Travel Tip

Our core values are important *road*SIGNS for the journey of life. They tell us which direction is aligned with our purpose, inform us of the speed limit, and guide our decision making. Without them, we become disoriented, a traveler nonetheless, but one without a sense of direction. Take time to consider what your big rocks are, those core values that allow you to be true to the one person who is the most important person of all—yourself.

Living Intentionally

*Stop ignoring the urge to get on with the work you should do
or to finally redefine a relationship: That whisper you keep hearing
is the universe trying to get your attention.*

Make it your intention *to pursue only what is honorable,
what is good, what is true—and the result will be a life
grander than you could ever have imagined.*
Oprah Winfrey, *O Magazine*, January 2002

I am prone to New Year's resolutions, setting goals, management by objectives
(MBO), creating endless numbers of "to do" lists—in other words, framing my life.

The typical new year begins the anticipation of what it will bring, followed by all the usual questions:

- *What do I want to accomplish this year?*
- *What is my calling/purpose?*
- *What am I being asked to contribute to the world?*
- *What surprises, losses or wake-up calls will I face?*
- *What do I need to do?*

Traditionally, I sit down at the beginning of each year to record my resolutions for the upcoming months, as I am sure many of you do, as well. I have become a skeptic when it comes to resolutions, however. They seem to be just another form of goal setting driving the "doing" part of my life. In trying to find the delicate balance between doing and being, I am wondering how resolutions serve me. I have decided that I need to approach this "resolution business" in a new way so that I address the issue of life balance differently. My solution is turn to **intentions** rather than to traditional resolutions.

You are probably thinking, "How are intentions different from resolutions?" In my understanding, intentions are an expression of who I want to become and how I wish to live. They differ from resolutions, as they are not linked to a specific outcome. An intention provides the opportunity for me to change a belief system or a pattern of behavior.

An example:

I might resolve to lose 10 pounds in the next two months or to quit smoking on New Year's Day. Both of these have fixed outcomes attached. By comparison, I might state that my intention is to be in excellent health. If I make a commitment to excellent health, and pay attention to my daily choices in supporting this intention, the results will follow.

Intentions can be stated in different ways. They may be questions: something I am seeking to understand (What is my life's purpose?), a statement that relates to how I wish to "be" in the world (I approach my life with joy and gratitude), or one of my core values that I wish to express more fully in life (I am loved and loving). An intention can also be something I wish to release, to let go of (I let go of fear). Finally, an intention may be a statement of what I wish to draw into my life (I want to do work that supports my Soul's Purpose in the service of others).

By stating intentions, we harness the energy that helps us to change our lives, one step at a time. We exercise full responsibility and accountability for who we are now and who we choose to become in the future. I encourage you to join me in recording your intentions. Write them down, in the present tense, and review them daily. Pay attention to what changes are occurring in your life. Listen. Observe. Begin to write intentions for all things you wish to change, remembering that, as Gandhi said, we must "be the change we wish to see in the world."

Travelogue

Journaling Questions

In her book *I Will Not Die an Unlived Life: Reclaiming Purpose and Passion*, Dawna Markova asks the following questions:

- What have I come here to give?
- What is unfinished for me to learn, to experience?
- Am I leaving a legacy that enables others to live bigger lives than I have? What is this legacy?

My Intentions

In my workshops, I ask participants to write down intentions throughout the day. It helps to practice. We discuss what it means to "live with intention," describing as clearly as possible the life experience we wish to have and then paying attention to the SIGNS, the things that inform us everyday in response to our intentions. Take a moment and write some intentions for yourself. Remember the guiding principles for intentions. They:

- are as precise as possible (A friend of mine formed the intention to attract more work. She did, but over the next year she failed to make more money. She needed to be more precise and state the intention of attracting more work and increasing her earning power.);
- can be stated as a question, something you want to attract, something you wish to release;

- have no specific outcome. If the outcome is defined in black and white, we do not trust our higher power. We are determining absolutely what we want and eliminating other possibilities, yet we do not always know what is in our highest and best interest.

Try the following, based on the exercises in the previous chapters: Return to the Being-Doing Continuum in "Road Liable to Subsidence" (page 15). Write an intention related to living a life in balance, the integration of doing and being.

From "The Big Rocks in My Life" (page 39), what were your core values? Write an intention related to aligning different aspects of your life with your core values.

From "Children Being Children" (page 31), what does your inner child know? Write an intention related to this.

Travel Tip

Ask yourself frequently, "Who am I?" and "What do I want?" Write down your answers. Form specific intentions related to your responses so that you can manifest the life you want. Remember these rules: "If you cannot name it, you cannot have it" and "If you can not see it, you cannot be it." Knowing what you want sets the direction for your life.

You're Not the Boss of Me!

Let those who believe in working toward forgiveness strive to
achieve it. Let those who believe it arrives through serendipity wait
for its appearance within. Let those of us who find certain things
unforgivable seek other paths to peace. And let us all find wholeness.
Laura Davis, *I Thought We'd Never Speak Again*

Just down the street from where I live, one of my neighbours posted the sign
"Cat Xing." The first time I saw it, I was reminded of a book by Warren
Bennis entitled *Herding Cats*. Of course the notion that we could ever herd cats
is a ridiculous one, as those of us who have lived with them know. They have a
mind and a will of their own. When it comes to people, though, we seem to

think that not only can we shape the beliefs and habits of others, it is our moral obligation to do so. Certainly this applies to raising children or grooming a spouse. Our oldest nephew, Owen, quickly reshaped this flawed thinking for all of us, rendering the idea of "herding people" as equally ridiculous. From the time Owen found his own voice, he could be heard saying, with great determination, "You are not the boss of me!"

This is not exactly what Owen's parents wanted to hear, but those of you who have pitted your will against that of your child, know that, indeed, we are not the boss of them. At the very best we can be "guides on the side," coaching them forward, offering advice or teaching them right from wrong. In the end, the only person who can be the boss of anyone is himself or herself. In the end, we are the only one at the helm of our own life.

For many of us, this lesson—being the boss of ourselves—comes late. We learn early to blame others for life's circumstances, avoiding the truth that we and only we are responsible for the life we are leading. I am certainly guilty. I was in my mid-twenties before I discovered that I was the boss of me. The great "aha" moment occurred during a retreat called People Searching Inward. This was my first foray into the inner world of self. I was already searching for greater meaning in my life. The experience was like waking up for the first time, realizing that I was one hundred percent responsible for defining my life and creating my reality in this world. It was huge, for it meant divesting myself of a suit of armor, built from the metal of blame I had worn for a very long time.

Oprah Winfrey closes her monthly magazine with her column entitled "What I Know for Sure." This always causes me to wonder what I know for sure and this is what I have discovered:

- I am the one and only boss of me.
- There is no one to blame for my circumstances or my choices but me.
- The only person in the world who can change me is me.
- It is not my job, nor can I, change others.
- When I see the truth of me—recognizing my strengths and my uniqueness—I manifest these more fully in my life.
- When I honor myself, I encourage others to do the same; I serve as a positive role model.

The idea that "I am the one and only boss of me" is both empowering and frightening. There is a moment in life when most of us realize that we are accountable and responsible for the quality of our life, both our successes and perceived failures, how we live, our relationships, and so on. The "aha" moment, when we own responsibility for ourselves, is the first major step in taking back our own power. It is also the first step in learning how to live the life we choose.

Many of us come from painful pasts. I am no exception. Growing up with an alcoholic father was, on most occasions, a nightmare. I blamed him for my not having close friends as I was growing up, for my timidity in public, for finding comfort in food and being overweight, and for most of the other woes in my life. Releasing this blame, something I continue to this day, has allowed me to breathe new vitality into my life every time I work on healing and forgiveness. I have come to embrace my past with gratitude, for it is my childhood experiences that allow me to have great compassion for others and to do the work I do.

In her recently published book, *I Thought We'd Never Speak Again: The Road from Estrangement to Reconciliation,* Laura Davis states that we come to a crossroads in our life when our focus naturally shifts to the present; when we recognize the price of holding on to a painful past. If we agree that I am the one and only boss of me, we need to ask:

- What is the price of holding on to a painful past?
- Is it a price we want to continue to pay?
- How is my past holding me back, preventing me from occupying my days in the present moment?

I invite you to take a closer look at who and what in your life you are blaming and how these thoughts are holding you captive, preventing you from inhabiting your days.

Travelogue

Journaling Questions
- What pain am I holding on to?
- What is the price of holding on to a painful past?

- What am I experiencing as a result of this pain (physical, emotional, spiritual)? Is it a price I want to continue to pay?
- How is my past preventing me from occupying my days in the present moment?

Create a Forgiveness List

In his book *Forgiveness: The Greatest Healer of All*, Gerald Jampolsky reminds us that to forgive does not imply that you agree with the lives or actions of others. Forgiveness is something we do for ourselves. It heals our heart. Bearing a grudge, refusing to release another from blame, does not make them feel bad, it makes us feel bad. It is that simple. In Jampolsky's words, "Forgiveness releases us from so much. It stops our inner battles with ourselves. It allows us to stop recycling anger and blame."

Who do you need to forgive? Take out a sheet of paper and write down all the names you can think of, everyone who has wronged you—family members, friends or colleagues.

Once the list is completed, take two or three of the people from the list and write down what they did or said to hurt you. Close your eyes. Taking each one of them, one person at a time, see them in your mind's eye, tell them you do not agree with what they did. Then, love them; surround them with warm radiant light. As you do so, allow the blame to dissipate; release it. Depending on who this is and how badly you were hurt, you may need to do this several times. That is okay. Work your way through the list, not all at once, but slowly. After a few days, notice how you are feeling. As you forgive, you take back your power, and shift into owning your life.

Travel Tip

Understand that you are free. Know that only YOU can choose the path YOU wish to follow. It is easy to blame others or circumstances for the things that happen in our life. We believe that others are determining the direction we are taking or placing the obstacles we cannot seem to surmount. We invest energy into emotions such as anger, envy, why me? Unfortunately, blame only defers responsibility. We fail to see the *road*SIGNS and, subsequently, fail to learn the lessons we are being called to learn. When we understand that we are free to choose and to assume self-responsibility for our life journey, we release the negative energy that keeps us in low gear. It is time to examine where in our lives we are not taking responsibility and to understand the consequences. It is time to release anger and blame, and to accept that we are free to choose our own authentic path.

Finding True North

~ True North Principles ~

The most fundamental source and the root of all the rest, one that can absolutely be relied on in any given set of circumstances, is our adherence to a set of changeless principles. This means constantly educating and obeying our conscience. The more we do these things, the greater will be our happiness…and the more we will be given wisdom and guidance and power in solving or transcending the various problems and challenges we encounter.
Stephen R. Covey, *Principle-Centered Leadership*

I love spring and all that this season brings with it—new growth, longer days, warmer temperatures, spring flowers and, of course, geese filling the sky, returning to their summer homes. My eyes are constantly drawn upward as the sun rises and sets and the distant chorus of honking puts me on notice that thousands of migrating snow and Canada geese are about to fill the sky over our home. How quickly their "V"s of flight form, called northward by an age-old instinct. There is no hesitation in those early moments of flight; they know where they are going, who their traveling companions are, what direction their journey will take, and where their eventual destination lies.

The story of the goose has been told and retold in teamwork literature, but there is a greater message encoded in their behavior that calls to me. The goose does not take flight in a directionless path; he knows where his True North lies. Informed by all the signs in his life, the length of the day and the changing temperatures, each bird takes to the sky and flies thousands of miles from his winter home to his summer habitat. It is an arduous and dangerous path, yet the goose is not deterred. Each morning he rises with the sun and the morning air currents and heads ever northward, occasionally stopping to rest in different staging areas, forage for food and take time to refuel before continuing the last lap of his journey.

As the geese fly overhead, I feel a tinge of envy. I wish I had such absolute instinct and sense of direction, that knowing of where my True North lies. I wish I had the presence to see, hear and allow the signs in my life to inform me of my destiny and my call to service.

Each spring, when I take the time to stop and listen, I see that the goose teaches me many lessons:

Commitment—rising each day at dawn, taking flight and staying the course;

Courage—moving forward no matter what the circumstances, traveling through rain, snow, sleet, often near starvation;

Purpose—absolute knowledge of the direction he is heading, never straying far from his course;

Community—traveling with others, supporting and encouraging an entire flock with his incessant honking.

Some would say the goose is simply programmed to fly north each spring by its genetic coding. I will not disagree with this view. But I still ask myself—and ask you—can we as human beings not learn from their commitment, courage, purpose and sense of community and apply these lessons to ourselves? If we did so, would we not be more successful in terms of living on purpose. Called constantly to our own sense of True North, we would define our own unique place in the world, know our destiny and understand our call to service. We would use this vision, along with our core values, as guideposts to our daily activity and actions. We might occasionally stray off-course, to explore or forage, but we would be called back eventually to resume our journey northward. We would see the signs in our life, those daily synchronicities that we are generally unaware of.

Travelogue

Seeing the SIGNS

Unless we pay attention, we do not see the SIGNS in our life. Over the

next week, start paying more attention. What are you looking for? Here are some suggestions:

- Listen more deeply to conversations you overhear or participate in. What are you hearing that seems to be specifically meant for you? What words? What emotions do these words evoke?
- Observe those around you more closely, noting interactions and incidents. What do you find yourself responding to? What are you seeing, beyond the obvious? What are these incidents telling you?
- Be watchful for synchronicities. There is no such thing as a coincidence. Why do some people cross your path? Why do certain things happen? What do these synchronicities call you to learn?
- When listening to the radio or watching TV, be aware of what catches your attention. What feels toxic? What brings you joy, makes you tingle inside? What makes you feel the emotion rise up in your chest?
- Observe all the signs you see while driving to and from different meetings. What are they telling you?
- What are you doing each day that so captures your attention that you lose all sense of time passing? How does that feel?
- At the end of each day, reflect on all that happened. What were you doing during those moments in which you felt most connected to you?

At the end of each day, take 10 minutes and make a few notes in response to these questions. At the end of the week, read the notes. Notice what trends you see.

SIGNS take many forms, but unless we pay attention, think about them and seek to understand them, we are not allowing them to inform us of our True North.

Journaling Questions
- What makes you unique (specific talents, strengths, gifts)?
- In what ways are you called to use your talents, to serve?
- Make a list of your unique qualities and the contributions you wish to make in this lifetime. Keep the list with you and review it daily. Begin to define your True North.

Travel Tip

Make a commitment to rise each day, take flight and follow your own path. Acknowledge and celebrate your uniqueness, and have the courage to live your life as you choose. Embrace your sense of purpose, that sense of what is right buried deep within, and let this be your guide as you negotiate through the maze of highways and byways each day. Live a life of service, loving yourself first and letting this love spill out to others within your community. Take note of the SIGNS which inform you of your True North. When you are pulled off-course by events or people, do not loose heart. Pick yourself up, take a deep breath, and remind yourself where True North lies. Set your course again.

Two Kinds of Tired

We who lived in the concentration camps can remember the men who walked through the huts comforting others, giving away their last piece of bread. They may have been few in number, but they offer sufficient proof that everything can be taken away but one thing: the last of the human freedoms—to choose one's attitude in any given set of circumstances, to choose one's own way.
Viktor Frankl, *Man's Search for Meaning*

One of my all-time favourite songwriter/storytellers was Harry Chapin. He left this world too soon, a troubadour and servant, sharing his wisdom in his concerts and raising money and awareness regarding issues of world hunger. I often find myself listening to his music, a great companion for a drive in the country.

On one of his "greatest hits" recordings, he speaks about his grandfather, the stories he told and the wisdom he imparted. He said, "My grandfather always used to say, 'Harry, in this world there are two kinds of tired—good tired and bad tired.'" The words resonated with me as I remembered both the good and bad tired moments of my life. These days, I am grateful to be mostly "good tired."

"Bad tired" can follow a day when you are seen as a winner in the eyes of others, but you know that you won other people's battles or lived other people's days, other people's agendas and other people's dreams. You achieved great things but for someone else's cause. At the end of the day, you see that there was very little of YOU in there. You realize that deep inside yourself, the parts are not connected. When you lay your head down that night, you toss and turn; you don't rest easy. You know your "doings" of the day are disconnected from your being, from your core values and from your sense of purpose.

Then there are the days when you are "good tired." Good tired can be the result of a day in which you experience less success, trying but not always satisfied with the outcome. The key is that you are working at the things you truly love and enjoy. You don't need to be hard on yourself because you know that you fought your own battles, you chased your own dreams, and you lived your days fully. This path is sometimes more difficult, but you feel better about yourself because your choices are in-line with who you are and what you believe in. At the end of the day when you lay down your head, you rest easy. You know that what you did that day, what you achieved, was connected to your purpose and values.

If you examine your days at their close, are you good tired or bad tired? Is what you do, what you are trying to achieve, connected to who you are—your being, your values, your purpose?

I am sure that all of us experience days when we are bad tired and others when we are good tired. Bad tired is being exhausted because what we are doing steals our energy and power. It may be the work we are doing, it may be the environment we do it in, or it may be the people we are spending time with. Whatever the cause, we become disconnected from our essence. The days end in fatigue and disillusionment; we feel empty inside. Our sense of achievement is overshadowed as we are not sure that what we did that day had any real meaning for anyone.

Good tired is about having a deep sense of satisfaction. It is about living a life of meaning and sensing that what we are doing is of value and valued. We want to know that, in some small way, we are making a difference to someone, whether the recipient is miles away or sitting next to us. We want to know that what we do does not harm other people or the planet.

All of us have the capacity to serve in a significant way, whether we repair appliances, write computer programs, teach courses or drive buses. It is simply a choice that we make. If we are feeling bad tired, we need to identify why and understand that the solution lies within us. It may mean a change in our place of work, our career path or how we live. Or it may be as straightforward as taking the time to find the meaning in what we are currently doing, reconnecting with our values and purpose and seeing the abundance in our lives.

Travelogue

A Great Day at Work

There are moments in our work lives when everything seems to go right, when we are deriving great pleasure from what we are doing and who we are being. Sometimes we even describe these moments as blissful. Kahil Gibran expressed it in the following way: "Work is love made visible." Take a moment and reflect on when you have had such an experience within your work environment. Record on Post-it Notes how you would describe this day, writing only one idea per note. As you record your thoughts, begin to post these notes in front of you, creating a storyboard of your "good tired" day. Write as many descriptors as you can, exhausting all possibilities.

Now, review all your Post-it Notes and categorize them under the headings of Mastery, Community and Service:

Mastery—your ability to apply your knowledge appropriately, work on a project and have a sense of achievement or learn something new;

Community—a sense of chemistry, that things are "clicking" well between you and your colleagues, resulting in great work and camaraderie;

Service—a sense that what you are doing makes a difference for one of your customers, either internal or external.

Once you have completed this exercise, note the category in which most of your descriptors are posted. Are the majority under Mastery, Community or

Service? Your "good tired" day needs to honor what you view as important to you in terms of your sense of well-being. If you examine your current work environment, do you have the opportunity to experience all three of these important aspects of work in a balanced way? If you have a strong need for community, is that evident in your workplace? What is missing? What steps can you take to create what you need at work?

Journaling Question
- What are you doing, when you lose all sense of time, when you feel connected body, mind and spirit?

Travel Tip

Make a choice to be "good tired." Find ways of being connected to your own sense of mastery, what you do well. See how what you do makes a difference for others. No matter what job you perform, understand that no job is too small if your intention is to do good. Be guided by your sense of right and wrong, your ethical center and your BIG ROCKS. If your wheels are aligned, the going is smooth. You arrive tired but not exhausted.

PART 3

An Abundant Life

Everyday Abundance

When I surrendered my desire for security and sought serenity instead,
I looked at my life with open eyes. I saw that I had much for which to be
grateful. I felt humbled by my riches and regretted that I took for granted
the abundance that already existed in my life. How could I expect more
from the Universe when I didn't appreciate what I already had?
Sarah Ban Breathnach, *Simple Abundance*

The fall of each year is about celebrating abundance. It is the time of the harvest, the reaping of the benefits of another summer of labor. As we celebrate Thanksgiving—a feast of turkey, fall vegetables and pumpkin pie—we take time to remember and give thanks for the bounty in our lives.

In rural Canada, abundance surrounds us. Signs announcing which type of corn, wheat or other grain is being grown or which type of fertilizer is being used frame our local roads. In October, the tractors are out in the fields harvesting this year's crop, often working around the clock before our Canadian winter sets in. There is a certain rhythm to a farmer's life, a cycle of sowing and reaping. As I watch, I begin to wonder about what I sow and reap each day, each week or each season. And as I reflect, I remember the importance of seeing the abundance in my life and of expressing gratitude for what I see.

In her book *Simple Abundance*, Sarah Ban Breathnach suggests a powerful exercise called the Gratitude Journal. The journal is written everyday for 90 days as a way of capturing those things in our daily experience for which we are grateful. I decided to try this for myself.

During the three months of writing my daily gratitudes, I learned many lessons. First, I learned that it is easier to complain and blame than it is to express gratitude. I learned that I was living life from a scarcity point of view rather than one of abundance. I realized that it was easy to be grateful for all the wonderful things in my life but that I struggled to be grateful for life's difficulties, even though these have been my great lessons. I became more aware of the small things in life that make a difference—a morning sky filled with fuchsia and indigo, a hummingbird at our feeders, a snowy blustery day giving me permission to stay in bed, a shared meal with friends…

With practice, I began to see each of these things—the rich tapestry of my life. I began to inhabit my days in a new way. I grew to appreciate that even the most difficult of days were filled with moments which helped me grow, learn and evolve. I rediscovered my humor and creativity. And, most importantly, I realized that the more I found to be grateful for, the more wonderful things began to happen in my life. I was attracting positive energy to me. I was now living with a "cup half full to brimming" philosophy.

The daily discipline of writing about gratitude also gave me the time to remember. As a person who, in Jungian terminology, has a strong intuitive preference, I tend to live in the future, the land of possibility. I have difficulty being fully present in my life in the here and now. Journaling was, and continues to be, an important practice for anchoring me in the present. I was able to review my days and see what was really going on, to appreciate the SIGNS. I began to realize that when I sowed the seeds of gratitude, a harvest of abundance was there to reap.

Today I have a gratitude practice as part of my daily life. I no longer keep a gratitude journal, but before dinner each evening, instead of grace, Jim and I share our "gratitudes" for the day. When I am alone, I have a nightly discipline of reviewing my day just before I go to sleep. The consequence is that each day ends in gratitude. And this changes everything. What is your gratitude practice?

Travelogue

Journaling Questions

- What would you like to attract to your life?
- Where in your life do you have this now?
- In what ways are you expressing gratitude in your life?

A Practice of Gratitude

Today is the day to begin to shift the energy in your life from fear to love, from scarcity to abundance. One sure way of achieving this is to begin "a practice of gratitude." There are various ways of doing this:

- Begin to keep a Gratitude Journal. This journal should be used exclusively for this purpose. Make it a daily practice for a minimum of 90 days. Try to capture gratitude for both the positive things and the difficult situations that teach you the great lessons. Remember a time in the past, something heartfelt or hurtful. Write the lesson in gratitude. When the 90 days are over, reread your journal. Highlight repeating themes or the great "aha" moments.

- Begin every evening meal with a gratitude sharing. This is wonderful to teach children and a great way to get in touch with one another's day. Hold hands as you do it, touching one another, closing the circle for this sharing time.

- At work, end meetings by asking your colleagues to share something they are grateful for as a result of the meeting. I did this once with a group of 50 priests after facilitating a day-long "open space event" for them. It was very powerful and everyone left with a stronger sense of their community.

Travel Tip

Express gratitude often, for whatever crosses your path—a sunset, a butterfly, a rainbow, a "V" of geese taking flight at sunrise, a hug, a sincere expression of gratitude from another, a difficult lesson. When we express gratitude for something we cherish, we draw more of this energy to us and open ourselves to receiving.

Am I Feeding Myself a "Junk Food" Diet?

Being impeccable (with your word) is not going against yourself.
When you are impeccable you take responsibility for
your actions, but you do not judge or blame yourself.
Don Miguel Ruiz, *The Four Agreements*

When was the last time you listened in on a conversation you were having with yourself—really listened to that internal dialogue that runs in your head during the day or on your way home from work? You might be reflecting on what someone else said to you, how things went at work or how well you served a customer or interacted with a colleague.

When we really listen, we often find that the messages we are feeding ourselves are negative ones: the things we did not say or do right or things we could have done better. There are few, if any, affirming messages within the text. I refer to this as "junk food" for the spirit, that slippery slope of diminishing ourselves in our own eyes, whittling away at our self-esteem and undermining our confidence. We begin to suffer from spiritual malnutrition.

If we were suffering from other forms of malnutrition, we would address the problem by improving our diet. We might even pay closer attention to the five food groups within the Canada Food Guide. We know there is a simple cause and effect relationship; eat a balanced diet, feel better. What, then, do we need to feed ourselves to have a healthy spirit-full diet? I would like to propose the following, the five spiritual food groups I refer to as GRACE:

G = Gratitude. Gratitude is the first major food group. Gratitude is a life philosophy that recognizes the good things in our life. It means recognizing the abundance of our own uniqueness. A gratitude practice acknowledges the many lessons life has offered us, both good and bad, understanding that these experiences and life events have helped us develop into the people we are now. It is taking time, everyday, to say out loud, "Today I am grateful for…"

R = Responsibility. The second food group, responsibility, refers to owning our own power, of knowing that only I can be the boss of me. It is accepting that my choices, not someone else's, are what ultimately determine my path. Responsibility is about knowing what our sense of purpose is, defining our core values and living by these.

A = Awareness. Awareness, the third food group, is about knowing our-selves—our gifts, strengths, talents and knowledge. It is about applying this self-knowledge to what we do, finding opportunities to express our gifts in the world and developing a sense of our own mastery. Mastery is the Vitamin A for self-esteem and confidence.

C = Courage. The fourth food group, courage, is the "breakfast of champions." It means starting each day with intention and asking, "What do I want this day to be?" and "How do I wish to be of service to others?" Courage implies holding this focus throughout our day and not being undermined by the atti-tudes of others.

E = Enthusiasm. Our last food group, enthusiasm, means joyfully embracing life, living every moment of every day fully and being the best we can be. Enthusiasm allows us to show our light to the world and to model this for others. Simply put, it is having unconditional love for ourselves, and in doing so, opening ourselves to the possibility of receiving love from others.

My invitation to you is to start paying attention to your internal dialogue, your spiritual diet. Discern what is junk food and what is spirit-full, and make a conscious choice to choose from the five food groups of GRACE.

Travelogue

When Do I Shine Brightly? (Enhancing Our Awareness)

Identifying past achievements or accomplishments is key to understanding when and where you are successful in your endeavors. I refer to this as mastery: the skills, knowledge and expertise we draw upon when we are at our very best. When we feel masterful, our inner wisdom and brilliance shines through.

Mastery can be found at a time when:

- you were able to use your skills and knowledge to the best of your ability;
- you met and/or exceeded the expectations of others;
- you enjoyed applying your knowledge;
- you had inner feelings of self-satisfaction and self-worth.

To understand your life's accomplishments, you must first identify them. Start by creating a list of as many accomplishments you can think of. Do not limit yourself to work. Consider events that occurred throughout your life, in childhood and adulthood, in play and in work, with colleagues, friends and family. Identify as many accomplishments as you can.

Next, choose three of these accomplishments which were particularly meaningful to you. Note why this was so. Write a short story, a factual account of what happened, step by step, about each of these three accomplishments. As clearly as possible, create a picture of the actual event.

Share your stories with a learning partner. Have them listen without interruption, noting strategies you used, strengths you brought to the situation, the values that guided your decision making. After telling the three stories, note the common threads. What do these stories bring into your awareness that you may have overlooked previously?

Journaling Questions

- Listen carefully.
  What messages are you feeding yourself at the end of every day?
- Take time. Rewrite the script.
- When you begin to hear your "junk food" dialogue, stop yourself.
  Replace the message with what you want to hear about yourself.
- What messages do you want to be feeding yourself?
  Catch yourself doing wonderful things each day and feed
  these to your spirit.

Travel Tip

On the journey of life, we need fuel to stoke our passion and keep our spirit strong. We have a choice to make every time we gas up: low- or high-octane. The high-octane choice reminds us of our uniqueness and the contribution we make each day. It keeps our spirit fueled for the duration of the journey and allows us to appreciate the scenery. Make sure to check the quality of fuel you are putting in your spiritual tank. Choose only from the highest quality energy source.

Money Is Love

To make that leap of faith, we have to heal the
old mindsets that keep us separated from the
unlimited abundance of money in the world.
What's the trick? The trick is to reunite money
with its spiritual roots. to make money love.
Barbara Wilder, *Money Is Love*

Seeing life's abundance continues to be a challenging lesson for most of us, especially these days. Since the events of 9-11, we have witnessed declining market values and retirement plans with diminishing returns. I find myself responding, wanting to stockpile like a squirrel for a difficult winter ahead. My spirit knows this is not the answer, yet on those days when the news is particularly bad, I struggle to see the abundance of resources in my life. And of course, in return, the SIGNS continue to provide me with lessons related to my need to learn.

I travel a great deal, covering the highway between our home and either Montreal or Ottawa two to three times a week. Having a safe and reliable vehicle is important. When my faithful companion "Maxie" developed a thunderous noise one September day, I feared for her ongoing existence. She has seen me through a variety of traffic situations over the last six years and has been a steady and reliable road warrior. I was not prepared to lose her companionship! Off to the garage we went where she was diagnosed with a number of serious but manageable health problems: she needed a complete overhaul of her exhaust system, new brakes, plus the usual oil change and tune-up. All of this would cost a mere $1400.

Fourteen hundred dollars! I panicked for a moment, grappling with the idea of such a large sum of money for simple car repairs. Yes, my friend Maxie is worth it, but this will put a dent in the bank account. When I went to pay the bill, the Visa machine at the dealership would not process the transaction, something was wrong with their machine. My patience waning, I decided to go to the bank to withdraw the necessary amount. I was forced to come face to face with a teller and to hold the money in my hand. Electronic transfers seem so painless by comparison. Fourteen hundred dollars! My chest hurt and I couldn't breathe—so much money! Scarcity was staring me in the face once again.

A few weeks before, my friend Kerry had given me a book entitled *Money Is Love*. I guess she knew that I worried about money. Barbara Wilder, the author, explains that money is just energy. We can't have more of it unless we spend it or give it away to worthwhile causes. Money allows us to do good things for others. Hanging on to it, saving every penny, worrying about it, being miserly, does not enhance our relationship with money; it only perpetuates that scarcity point of view. As I read her words, my own sense of scarcity was confirmed.

One of the strategies Barbara Wilder suggests is to write "Money is love" on checks we issue. So here was my opportunity to practice. I could panic or I could shift gears and practice. As I approached the teller to make my cash withdrawal, I silently began to chant, "Money is love" in my head, like a meditation mantra. I walked up to the wicket.

Money is love. Money is love. The chorus rang just behind my ears. I exchanged the usual greetings with the teller and chatted about the weather and our hopes for the approaching weekend. She looked up from her papers. Her eyes landed on our company logo emblazoned on my shirt. She said, "Oh, that's interesting, what does it mean?" I explained a little a bit about *people*HEALTH and our company's mission, cultivating spirit and values in the workplace. "We sure need an injection of spirit these days," she commented. "Could you drop off a pamphlet about your work the next time you are in? We would be very interested." I smiled and indicated to her I would. *Money is love*,

I chanted silently, experiencing a new energy. Had my new-found attitude opened up a new business possibility for me, I wondered? Is it possible that understanding that MONEY IS LOVE is the door to opening all the abundance I can imagine in my life?

It seems to me that we spend far too much time and energy worrying about money. If we think money will be scarce, it will be. When we acknowledge the abundance in our lives, it will always be there. I am learning how to turn off the old programs, to be more generous, to open myself to receiving and to understand that "money is, simply put, an exchange of energy and, yes, love."

Travelogue

Journaling Questions
- Describe your relationship with money?
- What would you like to change about your relationship with money?
- Where will you begin?

The Shift From Scarcity to Abundance
There are a number of things we can do to shift our focus from scarcity to abundance. Here are a number of things you can begin to integrate into your day-to-day routine:

Have a daily "gratitude practice." See "Everyday Abundance" (page 69) for details.

With each check you write, inscribe "Money is love" in the memo section. When you pay for something with cash or credit card, say "Money is love" to yourself as the exchange is made.

Give to good causes. Take the time to assess the impact your investment will have. As Barbara Wilder suggests, give to more highly evolved people or organizations, those who see the spiritual nature of money and the impact it can have in our world.

Time is money. Create balance in your life by giving your time to a good cause or taking time out with a friend or family member.

Meditate or pray. Visualize, recognize and honor the abundance in your life by closing your eyes, taking the time to call in and acknowledge all the abundance in your life in the physical plane (material wealth), emotional plane (relationships) and spiritual plane (your great strengths and talents).

Begin each day with the following intention:
I open my self to receive,
and in receiving, I honor the abundance in my life.
I release what I no longer need.

Travel Tip

As we travel the highway of life, we are constantly faced with choices. If I take that road what will I miss? If I go the other direction, what will I gain or find? We can focus on the things we missed or focus on the things we find. We can focus on what we don't have or we can shift and focus on what we *do* have. An emphasis on gain, rather than loss, allows us to live abundantly.

PART 4

Navigating the Waters of Change

A Bumpy Ride

The way of life is a journey, a journey along a winding path....
If you want to live, you need to give yourself over to the way
of transition—to let go when life presents you with a time
of ending, to abandon yourself to the neutral zone when that is
where you find yourself, to seize the opportunity to make
a new beginning when that moment presents itself.
William Bridges, *The Way of Transition*

It seems that just when life gets comfortable and the road ahead seems smooth, suddenly the bumps appear and we are forced to turn in a different direction. A neighbor whom you have grown to know and enjoy tells you that he and his family are moving to another area. Your oldest son gets married. Your best friends inform you that they are about to divorce. Your boss indicates that the promotion you have been waiting for has finally been approved and you take on new responsibilities and challenges. One of your closest friends from high school passes away after a long illness.

Change comes in many forms. It can be reason for celebration, concern or sorrow. It can have great significance in terms of its impact or it can be a mere ripple in our daily experience of life. Each of us has our own unique response to change: some of us seek it, some of us avoid it. But what ever it is, change has an impact on us.

We are told that "change is the only constant" in life and that we have no choice but to get on with it. This platitude doesn't always help. Sometimes we wonder, "Why is this happening to me?" We begin to experience an unexpected sense of being lost, of having no sense of where to turn next. Those around us grow impatient and accuse us of being stuck, resistant to change.

Few of us understand that change causes a significant internal response, a chain reaction of emotions and thoughts. For every change in our life, something we have known comes to an end. Change, good or bad, imposes a new beginning on us, a beginning that often has little definition or no boundaries to it. And in between these two points, the endings and the new beginnings, lies a period of uncertainty, wonder, grieving—a time we call the neutral zone. Endings, neutral zone, new beginnings…William Bridges refers to this as transition, "the process of letting go of the way things used to be and then taking hold of the way they subsequently become."

Change is also a significant *road*SIGN, and yet how often do we give ourselves permission to stop and reflect on the impact it has on our life? At the pace most of us travel these days, we simply keep moving. We push our thoughts and feelings to the back burner, ignoring them, hoping that any disease we have will disappear. We avoid understanding our transition, our human response to change. We may also miss an opportunity.

Change, and subsequently transition, is a wonderful thing. It creates openings for us to learn and grow, and to breathe new life into who we are now and who we seek to become. To reap the potential benefit change offers us, we need to understand it, reflect on its impact, positive or negative, and consider how it pushes us to live more authentically in the world. Our challenge is as follows: to pay attention to the changes occurring in our life, to embrace them and understand them, to ask what are we losing and what are we gaining, to allow ourselves to both grieve and wonder, and in so doing, to learn from our experience and to love who we are. Is it time for YOU to start paying attention to the changes in your life?

Travelogue

Carrots, Eggs and Coffee

Jenna and her father stood in the kitchen. She was home for the weekend, a break away from her university studies. As they stood preparing breakfast together, Jenna complained to her father about college, how everything around her seemed to be changing and how difficult she found her life. Her father, sensitive to her mood and concerns, listened. He suspected she wanted to give up. He understood that doing so was not the answer. Being the kind of dad he was, he decided to prepare a lesson as her morning meal.

He filled three pots with water and placed each on the stove. He turned all three burners on high. Soon the pots came to a boil. In the first one he placed carrots, in the second he dropped two eggs, and in the last he stirred in ground coffee beans. He let them sit and boil, without saying a word.

Jenna, not known as the most patient person in the world, sucked her teeth, sighed, tapped her fingers but decided to humor her father. She wondered what he was up to now, knowing that something was about to happen. Twenty minutes later he turned off the burners. He fished the carrots out and placed them on a plate. He pulled the eggs from the pot and placed them a bowl. Then he ladled the coffee out into a large cup.

As he turned to her he asked, "Jenna darling, what do you see?"

"Carrots, eggs and coffee," she replied. He brought her closer and asked her to check the texture of the carrots. She did and noted that they were soft. He then asked her to take the egg and break it. She pealed off the shell to find a hard-boiled egg. Finally, he asked her to sip the coffee. She smiled as she tasted its rich aroma.

She looked at her father. Curiosity had replaced her impatience. She asked, "What does it mean, Father?" He explained that each of them had the same change imposed on them—boiling water—but each reacted differently. The carrot went in strong, hard and unrelenting, but after being subjected to the boiling water, it softened and became weak. The egg had been fragile. Its thin outer shell had protected its liquid interior, but after sitting in the boiling water, the egg had become hard. The ground coffee beans, however, were different. They became one with the water; once added, they changed it.

"Which are you?" he asked his daughter. "When change knocks on your door, how do you respond? Do you give in and become limp, do you grow hard and resist it, or do you become one with it? Are you a carrot, an egg or a coffee bean?"

This story asks us to examine how we respond to change. Make a note of some of the recent changes in your life, even some from the past. How have you typically responded to either small or significant changes? Do you give in and become soft and limp, feeling victimized by the events around you. Do you dig in your heels and say, "No way! I refuse to be affected by these events! I will not budge!" Or, do you try to understand the external world while at the same time observing your own response, your feelings and thoughts, in regard to change? Take a moment and ask if you are a carrot, an egg or a coffee bean. Which would you prefer to be? Which would serve you best?

Journaling Questions

- What have been the significant changes in your life recently?
- What has come to an end as the result of a change?
- Do you have a sense of the new beginning you wish to create? How is this informing you about your purpose?

Travel Tip

The road is not always a smooth one. There are bumps; there are right turns, left turns and U-turns; there are yields, stops and dead ends. All of these *road*SIGNS imply a change in direction or a change in speed. Take the time to understand what these signs mean before reaccelerating. Assess how a change in direction can open you to new possibilities. Become an explorer.

Dead Ends

What a journey! This process of growth and change takes us along an ever-changing road. Sometimes the way is hard and craggy. Sometimes we climb mountains. Sometimes we slide down the other side on a toboggan. Sometimes we rest. Sometimes we grope through the darkness. Sometimes we're blinded by sunlight. At times many may walk with us on the road; sometimes we feel nearly alone. Ever changing, always interesting, and always leading someplace better, someplace good. What a journey!
Melody Beattie, *Journey to the Heart*

In the previous chapter, I introduced the idea that for every change, there is a human response called transition, a process of endings, new beginnings and, in between, a creative zone for personal growth and exploration. Acknowledging that change has an impact on us is a first step. Understanding this, however, does not necessarily reassure us; we may still not know how to respond.

Transitions begin with endings, a recognition that certain things have changed—aspects of our life that we must release. Each of us responds differently to endings. Some of us deny that the change is happening and bury our heads in the closest sand pile. Others love change, seek it out and are enthusiastic cheerleaders encouraging others onward. Most of us, however, simply try to go with the flow and survive the changes the best way we know how, hoping to feel settled once again. What we want to avoid is the sense that endings are DEAD ENDS.

Endings can touch many different aspects in our lives: our relationships, the scope of responsibilities we have at work, our sense of control or authority, the physical space we occupy, our future aspirations or our sense of who we are. The key is to recognize what the endings actually are, to allow ourselves to grieve the loss if we need to, to acknowledge our feelings and thoughts, and then, give ourselves permission to let them go and move forward. Failure to recognize the endings can hold us back and may show up in our lives in ways that we had not expected: anger, depression, frustration, anxiety or blame.

While "completing our endings" sounds easy and straightforward, this is not always the case. The process of recognizing and releasing often requires a concrete strategy, such as journaling about the events, having a ceremonial burial of the losses, or simply talking about our feelings with a good friend or learning partner.

If you are working through a significant change in your life, you may wish to stop and consider the following questions and strategies:

1. What do I need to disengage from?

   We often allow our relationships and our work to define who we are. This is how we have come to know ourselves. When this changes, we are forced to disengage from our traditional view of ourselves—the roles we have played or positions we have occupied, how we have come to know ourselves. Our sense of self-confidence may be shaken. The changed circumstances, however, present us with an opportunity to accept ourselves simply for who we are, not what we do.

   Who am I when I am not doing?
   Who am I when I am not playing a specific role?

2. How do I channel my disenchantment?

   Change, especially when it is outside our control (which it generally is), can leave us feeling disenchanted. We can respond in a variety of ways; it is our choice. We can focus on how we have been "hard done by" (and assume the victim's stance) or we can take responsibility for ourselves and focus on the opportunities available to us. Taking responsibility allows us to learn and move forward.

   What gratitude do I have for this change in my life?
   What opportunities am I beginning to see?

3. How do I find my way in the midst of this sense of disorientation?

   As we complete our endings and let go of what we have known, we may feel lost and disoriented, not having a sense of where to turn or how to redirect our life. This is a normal, healthy response. Allowing ourselves to live in that place of disorientation for a while, allows new aspects of "who we are" to emerge. It is a time to review and reconnect with your purpose and your core values. These will guide you.

What is my purpose?
What are my core values?

Travelogue

Endings: What Am I Losing?

Use the following Table to assess what you believe you are losing in a change you are currently experiencing. This is an opportunity for you to acknowledge how you have been affected by the changes in your work environment or personal life. As you do this for yourself, take time to also consider how these changes may have affected others around you, for example, teams or groups within your organization, customers, family or friends.

Be as specific as possible about the endings in your life. This is part of the healing journey. Change does not always feel good, even though we know that endings open space for new opportunity. Take time to name your endings, mourn and celebrate the losses. Then you can release them and move forward.

WHAT AM I LOSING?	WHO IS AFFECTED?			
	Me	Colleagues	Family	Friends
Turf				
Physical Space				
Status				
Responsibility				
Authority				
Influence				
Relationships				
Memberships				
Work Routine				
Family Unit				
Opportunity				
Meaningful Work				
Promotion/Advancement				
Control of Personal Destiny				
Sense of Mastery				
Security				
Other (name it)				

Journaling Questions

Once your endings have been identified, try these questions:

- In what ways are the "endings" in your life forcing you to disengage from how you have always known yourself?
- What changes have occurred that are requiring you to redefine who you are?
- When you take a deeper look at the changes in your life, what opportunities are there?
- What are you learning about yourself?

Travel Tip

Every life journey will have some dead ends—times when we are forced to change direction or even retrace our steps. If we embrace the opportunity that comes with these endings, we have an opportunity to redirect our life in new ways and to re-evaluate how we wish to continue our travels. As we let go of our normal routes and habits, we open up the opportunity for exploring new terrain and seeing new sights. Both are the gateway to new learning and personal growth, and the possibility of living in a more authentic way.

Mixed Signals

*There are so many ways to work on the Circle of Influence—
to be a better listener, to be a more loving "marriage" partner, to be
a better student, to be a more cooperative and dedicated employee.*

*Sometimes the most proactive thing we can do is to be happy, just to
genuinely smile. Happiness, like unhappiness, is a proactive choice.
There are things, like the weather, that our Circle of Influence will never
include. But as proactive people, we can carry our own physical or social
weather with us. We can be happy and accept those things that at present
we can't control, while we focus our efforts on the things we can.*
Stephen Covey, *The Seven Habits of Highly Effective People*

Sometimes I see *road*SIGNS that simply baffle me. Like life, SIGNS can be confusing. We are bombarded with lots of messages and signals, from people and our environment. This is especially true when things around us are changing. My mother always used to tell me not to worry about such things. "Worrying about what is going to happen," she would say, "is simply a waste of energy, and besides, it does not change the outcome."

Despite her wise words, my mother still worried a lot, and I, like a dutiful daughter, followed in her footsteps. It has taken me years to realize that the only thing worry does for me is drain my energy and leave me breathless. I am determined to transform this habit into something more positive, especially as I experience change in my own life and coach others through the process of change and transition.

On my learning journey, I have begun to pay attention to how people, including myself, respond to change and experience transition. Two trends seem to emerge. The first group have the capacity to enumerate all the concerns they could possibly have related to any given change. These individuals experience a sense of feeling completely overwhelmed, of a great shadow looming above them. The change, major or minor, becomes more than it is, bigger than life. They spend energy wondering what's next, what others will say or how they will respond, what problems are going to arise, where this is all leading…and more. All of these issues seem very real to them; however, the reality is that they have little or no control over what the actual outcomes will be. They are trapped in what Stephen Covey has called their "Circle of Concern," that big black hole of worry. They have yet to learn that focusing on all their possible concerns and worries is an unproductive, highly reactive and energy-consuming place to exist.

The second group has learned to slow down and take a closer look at change. These individuals realize that there are a number of issues they can actually influence, things that they can do something about. They choose to *respond* to events with a concrete strategy rather than simply react. When projects or events seem too big, they break them into "chewable chunks" of doable bits. They choose to take responsibility, be proactive and define the specific actions they wish to take—each step of the way. In this way, they take back their power and work within what Stephen Covey refers to as their "Circle of Influence."

I am learning that grounded, proactive people focus their energies on their Circle of Influence, and as a result, they ease their way through change and transition. They find opportunities for learning and personal growth within any change/transition process. They assume responsibility for the things that they know they can personally influence or control. They focus on strengths before weaknesses, abundance before scarcity, and love before fear. They model accountability instead of blame, they seek solutions rather than ruminating about problems, and they focus on working things through with others rather than waiting to see what happens. While acknowledging the losses they will experience within their own transition, they also understand the Law of Abundance—that *nothing ever disappears from our life, it just takes on another form.*

In observing my own response to change, I have come to recognize that I can make a choice to be a victim or to be in charge. Whatever my choice, I can create my own experience of change and be the master of my own transition. You can also make this choice. Consider the following: When your energy is positive, focused and proactive, you place yourself in the driver's seat. When your energy is reactive, scattered and negative, you become a passenger. You forfeit your power as you allow someone else to give your life direction. Which choice will you make?

Travelogue

Journaling Questions
- What do you find yourself worrying about?
  Are these things that you can influence or control?
- In what ways does worrying drain your energy (physical symptoms, emotions)?
- What are the issues within your Circle of Influence?
- What concrete steps can you put in place to influence the changes in your life and move your transition forward?

The Balance Sheet
In the table on the next page, make a list of the Benefits (pros) and Drawbacks (cons) of either resisting or embracing change.

When completing the table, adhere to these rules:

- Work across each line, writing down one thing in each column before moving on.
- Each column must have the same number of items listed in it; otherwise, you will not be in balance.

You may wish to do this with another person, brainstorming ideas as you go.

Embracing Change		Resisting Change	
Benefits	Drawbacks	Benefits	Drawbacks

When you have completed your list (try to get at least 10 items in each column), return to the table and review each column. When you examine the benefits and drawbacks on each side of the equation, which list would serve you best; that is, if applied, which list would be in your best interest? Now, what do you want to do?

Travel Tip

Signals and signs are often confusing. The direction we need to take or the choice we need to make may not be clear. We worry about things outside our control, and our fuel gauge slides to empty. Refill your tank. Focus on the things you can do, can influence and can affect. Your mileage will improve and you will arrive at your destination feeling rested and fulfilled.

PART 5

Honor Thyself

Choosing My Travel Companions

One of the tasks of true friendship is to listen compassionately
and creatively to the hidden silences. Often secrets are not
revealed in words, they lie concealed in the silence between the
words or in the depth of what is unsayable between two people....

The depth and substance of a friendship mirrors itself in the
quality and shelter of the silence between two people.
John O'Donohue, *Anam Cara*

Two children walking side by side; the sign warns us of a school crossing just ahead. School days, a time of learning, of coming into the world, of growing up, of forming relationships with others. We are molded and scolded by our teachers and parents, but it is our friends who influence us, hopefully love us and accept us, and whom we come to rely on and grow up with.

Relationships can either sustain us or drain us. Sometimes we are a poor judge of character and find ourselves attracted to people who claim to be our friends but who disappear in foul weather. Other times, we are drawn to people who are loving and caring and accept us, warts and all, for exactly who we are. Eventually we begin to realize that it is important to discern the friends with whom we wish to travel and share our time.

What is the quality of your adult relationships? Do you ever take time to assess how you spend your time and with whom? Adult friendships and learning relationships are an important part of our life. I do not refer here to acquaintances. Friendship, in this context, is founded on a deeper sense of knowing another person and caring for them unconditionally. They are people with whom you choose to spend quality time, who share a part of themselves with you, and who you can confide in and trust. These are relationships where both parties are fully present for one another.

When we allow ourselves to experience friendship in this way, we are inviting these friends to be with us as learning partners. When we make the choice to follow the spiritual path in our lives—a desire to be connected in body, mind and spirit—we need to find others with whom to share the journey. These special individuals choose to share their personal journey with us and we with them. As friends and learning partners, we see the potential in one another and challenge each other accordingly. We know we are safe in being ourselves, because our relationship is based on loving intention, unconditional love and compassion for one another. We are invested in one another's success in living "on purpose."

When we choose our learning partners, we need to do so carefully. Too often we surround ourselves with colleagues and friends who drain us of energy. I refer to these folk as the "energy vampires." They quite literally suck the life out of us. We find ourselves losing our personal power in these relationships, allowing our energy to be pulled from us like water through a sieve. Why do we do this? We know that the quality of any relationship has an influence on how we feel about ourselves. It is time to be watchful for the critics and judges, those who show up in our lives but who are not really present, or those who seek us out for their own needs but who give nothing in return. While we cannot eliminate them from our lives, we can limit the amount of time we give to them.

Make a choice to draw others to you in an intentional way. Know who these people are, the people you would like to have in your life. Decide that you can attract to you the kind of people who make you feel good about yourself, who you can enjoy and relax with. These are the friends who support you and who you can support in return—the ones who nurture your spirit and respect and honor who you are, without trying to change you. These are the friends who hold the mirror up for you, and reflect back to you the limits of your current path and choices. They challenge you to confront your fears and to live from love. They help clear the path when the going gets tough, but are also willing to throw plops of manure in your way to force you to reconsider a choice.

In her book *Return to Love*, Marianne Williamson describes learning partnerships as "assignments, part of the journey to inner knowing." We are in each other's lives in order to help one another assess and learn from life's lessons, to challenge one another to release life's wounds and to heal and support one another in the process. A learning partner—be it your life partner, a friend, a family member, a work colleague, even a family pet—is there to both support and challenge you, as a friend, mentor and coach, as you negotiate the twists and turns in the journey of your life.

It is important, in life, to surround ourselves with love. Yes, love comes from within, but we also need it without. Why would we choose to be drained by a friendship when we can make the choice to be filled by it? Is it time for you to assess who you spend your time with and who, among your friends, are the energy vampires and the energy boosters? Choose your friends and learning partners carefully.

Travelogue

My Spiritual Bank Account

Everyday we make choices for our spiritual well-being. If we begin to view our spiritual life as a bank account, we immediately recognize that our daily choices are either spiritual deposits or withdrawals. We hope that at the end of each day we have an outstanding balance that is healthy and able to provide us with the spiritual sustenance we need. Read the statements below which capture the different ways we make both deposits and withdrawals. Tick off the boxes beside the ones that you most agree with. When you have read and responded to all statements, add up both columns.

Spiritual Deposits		Spiritual Withdrawals	
I have relationships that fill me up with love and nurture my spirit.		I have friendships which drain me and leave me feeling empty inside.	
I am clear about my own priorities, what works for me. I know when to say "no."		I live by what others expect of me. I have trouble saying "no."	
I take responsibility for my issues and my life. I am the "boss of me."		I feel that I have little or no control over what happens to me.	
I actively work at forgiveness. I know that forgiveness does not mean that I agree with the choices of others.		I cannot seem to forgive those who have harmed me, and I continue to blame them.	
I search for or create physical environments that make me feel safe.		I allow clutter to accumulate. I sometimes feel as if I am suffocating.	

I live intentionally, defining how I wish to experience my life.	I worry about the "what if"s, "must do"s, and what others will think.	
I have a strong sense of my life purpose and core values. I use these as my *road*SIGNS for life.	I have no idea why I am here or what it is I am destined to do. I hesitate to make such a commitment.	
I take time to recharge my battery. I have a daily practice of meditation or prayer, journaling, or simply quiet time for me.	Every hour of every day is filled with something to do. I prefer to keep myself occupied most of the time.	
I see the many changes in my life as positive, an opportunity to stretch, learn and grow as a person.	I do not like change and find myself resisting it. I am afraid of trying things which are new, for fear I might fail.	
I work in an environment where my strengths and my spirit are appreciated. We celebrate our successes.	My work environment is spiritually toxic. Good work is rarely acknowledged. I feel more like a number than a person.	
Total	Total	

Is your spiritual bank account in balance, do you have a healthy surplus or are you overdrawn? What "spiritual withdrawals" do you want to address? What is your plan?

Journaling Questions
- What are some of the lessons you are seeking to learn at the moment?
- Who do you have around you to assist you with these lessons? How do they both challenge and support your learning?
- Who are the energy vampires in your life? What do you want to do about them?

Travel Tip

Choose your traveling companions well: those who nurture your spirit and honor your gifts, those who love you unconditionally, those who support *and* challenge you, and those with whom you love to spend time. These are your rightful travel companions.

A Life Lived Only Once Is a Life Unlived

Most of us would be secretly thrilled to have our life stories written,
yet we shy away from the attention. We see men and women being
interviewed on television or in magazines, but somehow we don't think
that we, too, have interesting stories to tell and valuable ideas to share.
On the contrary. Each of us has unique stories to tell.
Victoria Ryce, *By Me, About Me*

I recently read a wonderful novel. *Downhill Chance,* by Donna Morrissey, is a
story about the outports of Newfoundland during and immediately after
World War II. The author wrote of a rural and isolated life, free of any influence from the outside world, although all evidence suggested this was about to
change. This was a world where history was passed from one generation to

another through the spoken word, the art of storytelling and song. Without these stories, one generation would have known little of their family history. Likewise, they would learn little of the hardships or the heartache of growing up in less-than-ideal conditions.

In her book, Morrissey writes, "a life lived only once is a life unlived," recognizing that when we hold all our stories inside of us, they go to the grave with us. The bad memories can imprison and torment us; the good memories are simply locked away untold. Storytelling is a significant ingredient in a life well lived, key to both our learning and our healing. When we do not speak of our past, we steal from others the opportunity to share our experience. But when we do speak, we inhabit our days differently; we relive, revisit and see things differently; we remember, release, forgive and heal as others listen to us. It is in this process that we find our own voice.

The SIGN for the local library reminds us that we all have stories inside of us. These are the stories describing our family history: where we came from, our ancestry and our family traditions. They are the stories of a life lived: our childhood, our experiences, raising a family, having a career, the span of decades and our accumulated wisdom. They are the stories that teach a lesson: something our grandmother taught us, a favorite book, a parable or simply a fond memory. Whatever the stories are, I believe we need to create opportunities to tell them in writing or, more importantly, in storytelling circles. Our stories are our legacy, the life we created and the many ways in which we have served others; they provide our children and grandchildren with the roots to their past and the wings to their future.

For example:

I am the grandchild of a seafaring man, a captain of a tall ship which sailed from the Upper Lehave River, in Lunenburg County, Nova Scotia. His name was Aden Conrod, born of German heritage, the name changed over the years from Koonrod. He was a descendent of what the locals referred to as the Lunenburg Deutsch, a cohort of immigrants who landed in the new world sometime in the seventeenth century, who, like so many before them, were escaping religious persecution in their homeland.

He sailed each winter for the West Indies, trading molasses and brown sugar in exchange for lumber, ice and Nova Scotia Christmas trees. Some say he also imported rum, although the customs agents and RCMP awaited him each spring expecting to find an illegal cargo of some foreign spirits.

My mother said that the brown sugar danced when you opened up the barrels and the molasses was the best blackstrap to be found, thick and rich and laden with iron. It was the magic elixir that cured all ailments; it was the ingredient that found its way into the loaf of bread or a pot of homemade beans; it was served over porridge or a simple slice of white bread. A molasses jar always sat in the center of the dining room table, along with a cup of teaspoons for dipping.

Years later, when I was a child, molasses was still the sweetener of choice; warm milk laced with this dark brown syrup was our favorite bedtime drink.

I never met my grandfather; he died long before I was born, cancer stealing the breath from his lungs. I bless my mother for she drew pictures with her words, telling me the tales of this old salty dog; her brother Felix, a fur trader in Baffin Island who died mysteriously in this cold, dark place; her mother Ida who lived to see her first grandson, my brother, born; and her deceased siblings Ismay and Waldo. Without these stories I would have no knowledge of this family, who exists now only in my memory of my mother's words; a few birth records, the only written evidence of these people who lived so long ago.

Betty Healey, My Memories

Everything I know about my family was told to me by my mother and I thank her now for the gift of these stories. She died too young but left me a sense of history and legacy for which I shall always be grateful. While I have no children to whom to pass on these stories, I plan to bend my nephews' ears on a few occasions, so they, too, will know of their past.

Life has changed from the "good old days." As the twilight turns to night, we no longer sit around the dining-room table recalling the day's events, sharing what's important to us or our recollections of the past. Television has claimed our evenings and stolen our words from us. We rarely write letters to friends or family any longer, e-mail replacing "snail" mail. While no one can deny that these technological conveniences have improved some aspects of our lives, we need reminding that they do not replace folklore or family tale, the color of ink traced across a few pages in a familiar hand or the warm feeling we have in our belly as we sit with friends and listen to the tales unfold.

Telling our stories is a spiritual massage, freeing ourselves of painful memory and filling up with the abundance and wonder of our life. They create a vibrant multi-dimensional tapestry of who we are and where we have been. Our stories reflect and portray our authentic being.

My dream is that we begin to rekindle the tradition of oral storytelling, to encourage, model and practice it. This simple tool offers us the opportunity to reconnect families and communities and to enhance the human spirit. Each summer, our family gathers at my sister-in-law's cottage for our family reunion. There are many rituals associated with this event, of which storytelling is one. In the past, the stories have been shared primarily amongst our generation (my husband's brothers and sisters), but more recently, members of the next generation have begun listening in and participating. Laughter is always in great evidence, as are the tears when we reminisce about some of the sadder occasions. The important thing is that the stories keep the family fire aglow, the memories fanning the flames, the next generation embraced by a sense of where they came from.

We need these traditions both in our families and in our place of work. I encourage each of you to find your own voice, to tell your stories and to encourage others to do the same. I invite each of you back to the circle.

Travelogue

Telling Your Story

What is the story inside you that is burning to be told? Give yourself half an hour and write three pages, non-stop, about this story. Start with *I remember…*. See what happens. As you write, try using this technique suggested by Nathalie Goldberg in *Writing Down the Bones*:

- Start writing and keep your hand moving until the three pages are filled. This may mean writing "I don't know what to say." That is okay, just do not stop.
- Do not cross out words or worry about punctuation, spelling or grammar. Adjustments can come later. Just get what is inside *out* on paper.
- Let go and lose control. No one is watching. Write for yourself, not for someone else. This is your story. Tell it any way you want to.
- Don't think too much. There is no need to be logical. Write from your heart, from your gut.
- If something unexpected comes up in your writing, do not withdraw. Allow yourself to be naked and raw. Sometimes stories bring up a painful memory; that's okay. These allow us to heal.
- Get as many details as you can on paper. Be descriptive, not vague.

Once the story is written, share it, read it out loud. Before you read, ask the listener to not judge your writing, just listen deeply to the story. This is not about writing a masterpiece, it is about allowing the stories, some buried for too long, to come to the surface. Reading is different from writing and has its own healing power. Giving voice to your words allows you to hear the story yourself, to share it and release it.

Journaling Questions

Think of a story that was told to you by another person that deeply touched you.

- What was the message that resonated with you? What difference did it make for you?
- When was the last time you shared a personal story? How did that feel? How did it affect others?

Travel Tip

Share your stories with others as you travel. Take time to listen to the stories of your companions, as well. Buried in the text of any story lies great wisdom and opportunities for learning and healing. Stories provide fuel for our sometimes-empty tank.

Wedding Window – My Marriage Vows

I used to feel like I was waiting for someone to discover me,
to "produce" me, like Lana Turner at the drugstore.
Ultimately I realize the person I was waiting for was myself.
If we wait for the world's permission to shine, we will never receive it.
Marianne Williamson, *Return to Love*

"Goin' to the chapel and we're gonna get married…" The refrain of that old song plays in my head as the sign WEDDING WINDOW comes into view. I have been married now for almost 30 years. When I take a moment and think back to that day when I walked down the aisle, I am somewhat in awe of how willing I was to commit myself to spending a lifetime with another person. Although I did not take the commitment lightly, as marriage was in my view a lifelong contract, I readily vowed to love, cherish and honor this person with all my heart and spirit. Did I really know this other person, and more importantly, was I seasoned enough to really know what I wanted in a life partner?

If we are fortunate (and I know I am), our first choice in a partner will be a good one. The relationship not only lasts, it flourishes over time. The statistics tell us, however, that 50 percent of relationships fail. Why? Is it that we don't know what we want in a partner, or is it that we don't know ourselves? Perhaps relationships fail because we commit to do for others what we cannot do for ourselves first. When did we vow to love, cherish and honor ourselves? Imagine starting our adult lives with such a vow. I, Betty, take me Betty, to love and to cherish, to honor and to respect, until death do we part. What would happen if we put ourselves first, honoring the person we are, cherishing our spirit and loving ourselves unconditionally? In what ways would this change or redirect our lives?

I have decided that it is not too late, that I can choose to marry myself today: to reconnect with the person I have grown into (and who continues to change in subtle ways everyday), to see the abundance of my gifts and talents, and to celebrate me. I was discussing this with my friend and kindred spirit Kerry Messer last summer while we were in Taos, New Mexico, on retreat. Kerry agreed, and in one of her journals, she decided to take up the mantle and write her wedding vows. I was enormously touched when I first heard Kerry read these aloud and am grateful she has allowed me to share them here.

My Wedding Vows
Kerry Messer

I vow to hold myself in only the highest regard, to not put myself down or in anyway demean myself.

I vow to take responsibility for all my actions, but not to take on the responsibility for others' actions.

I vow to follow my heart and spirit wherever they might take me.

I vow to listen to my heart with stethoscope-like precision and trust my instincts under all circumstances.

I vow to surrender my need for control and to exert my will (no matter how well intentioned) and to let God's will drive my car through this life like she has in all my past lives.

I vow to be gentle and understanding of myself when I make mistakes.

I vow to forgive myself with grace and ease...to forgive all who have hurt or betrayed me or made mistakes that have affected me.

I vow to wake up every morning walking into the day remembering there is only now.

I vow to remember that I can't change the past or predetermine the future, but I can make the best choices for my higher good in the many moments of today.

I vow to take care of my body and health as if I was carrying myself as a fetus.

I vow to put no other before myself and my highest good.

In the book *Attracting Genuine Love*, authors Gay and Kathlyn Hendricks write that the first step in attracting love is to be in love with ourselves. "People who don't love themselves attract people who don't love themselves. When you love yourself, deeply and unconditionally and for everything you are and aren't, you attract people who love themselves. Then your relationships become partnerships on the path of love."

It is a difficult lesson to learn that we must love, honor and cherish ourselves first. We look to others to give us love, yet even when they do, this love falls on barren ground and cannot take root, for the soil has not been prepared to receive these love seeds. The idea of marrying ourselves first is an important step in self-love, accepting ourselves and assuming our own power. Are you willing to do your work, to write your vows and marry yourself first? Are you ready to vow to love, cherish and honor yourself?

Travelogue

Journaling Questions
- How do you love yourself? Count the ways. (If you can't identify any ways, what can you start doing today that will change that?)
- If you could marry yourself, what would your vows be?
  Write them down (or borrow Kerry's).
  Recite them to yourself in the mirror.
  How did that feel?

A Marriage Contract

Marriage begins with a contract with you—a commitment to love, honor and cherish the person you are. Take a moment and read through the marriage contract below. Fill in the things you love about yourself, along with your strengths, gifts and talents.

My Marriage Contract

I, _____, commit to loving myself unconditionally. What I love most about me is: _____

_____

_____

I cherish my great gifts and talents which show up in my life everyday. (List all the strengths, gifts and talents that make you who you are.)

_____

_____

_____

I pledge to honor these everyday. I am committed to my Core Values and allow these to guide my spirit. (List your core values from "Big Rocks.")

_____

_____

_____

Next, form an intention.

I _____, am worthy of being loved. I attract friends, who love me unconditionally, who honour and respect me, and who cherish me everyday. I attract the perfect partner, a person who loves me unconditionally, who honors and respects me, and who cherishes me every-day.

Create your own marriage contract on a beautiful piece of parchment, along with your wedding vows, and put in these a place where they will be visible to you everyday. This is your love letter to YOU and a daily reminder that you deserve to be loved.

Travel Tip

For nighttime travel, we turn on our headlights so that we can illuminate the road ahead. We need to do the same for our journey through life: turn the head-lights on and illuminate ourselves. Take a look at the abundance that has been given to you—your talents, your great strengths and the integrity of who you are. Love, honor and cherish your only lifelong traveling companion, YOU.

Peace

We have to make peace an attitude. Then we have to make it a habit. Finally, we must decide to live peace, to share it around the world—not just talk about it. We each have an equal purpose, whether that purpose is big or small...
Mattie Stepanek, *O Magazine*, November 2002

I find myself thinking about peace a lot, especially given the state of our world—the threat of war, the ongoing violence, and the lack of respect I see for human life. As I reflect on this, I find myself asking what can I do, what is my responsibility? The question is huge and I feel very small. As a single human being, I wonder how I can influence the events of the world, how I can contribute to peace.

In my heart, I know that peace begins with me. It starts by loving me and respecting the gifts that I bring to the world in my own unique way. Caroline Myss, in her book *Sacred Contracts*, refers to this as living our divine potential. "It is discovering the depths of your capacity to create and express love, compassion, generosity and wisdom….your potential motivates you to discover greater purpose and meaning to your life."

If we wish to see peace on earth, we need not look to the world leaders or our governments for the solution; we need to look to ourselves and ask how we can make a difference through each step we take, each interaction we have. Each of us is an instrument of "peace on earth." Imagine the world we can create together if each of us takes responsibility for finding the peace within and shining this into the world.

I extend to you the following invitation to:

- stop, look within, and define all the things that make you unique and special;
- live your divine potential;
- place your arms around yourself and give yourself an embrace like no other you have ever given yourself;
- be at peace in your heart—and ask yourself who are you blaming for something, who are you angry with, who has wronged you. Let it go. Forgive them, and in the forgiving, allow your light to shine even brighter;

- find a kinder, gentler way to communicate and to tell truth. Pay attention to the words you use, how you speak to others and your body language. As Charles Handy said, "our words are the dress of our thoughts";
- look around you for opportunities to make a difference for others. Practice random acts of kindness, start saying "thank you," tell others what wonderful things you see them doing everyday;
- start each day with an intention to make the world a better place, a place where love is the way.

This is the foundation of peace. If each one of us takes the time to see the light within ourselves and to turn up the dimmer switch, if we make the commitment to connect with others in a positive caring way, peace can no longer elude us. Now is the time to give the most important gift of all: LOVE.

Travelogue

The Weight of Nothing

"Tell me the weight of a snowflake," a coal mouse asked a white dove. "Nothing more than nothing," was the answer.

"In that case I must tell you a marvelous story," the coal mouse said. "I sat on the branch of a fir, close to its trunk, when it began to snow. Since I didn't have anything better to do, I counted the snowflakes settling on the twigs and needles of my branch. The number was exactly 3,741,952. When the next snowflake dropped onto the branch—nothing more than nothing, as you say—the branch broke off."

The dove, since Noah's time an authority on the matter, thought about the story for awhile and finally said to herself: "Perhaps there is only one person's voice lacking for peace to come about in the world."

Journaling Questions
- What choices are you making each day to bring peace to the world?
- Make a list of things you can do for your family, friends and colleagues at work that will make a difference for them. Now, do these things.

Travel Tip

Everyday we have a choice to make: to walk the path of love, light and peace or the path of fear, darkness and violence. As Robert Frost encouraged us, take the road less traveled—the path of love, light and peace. These three core values are the essential spark plugs of a powerful engine; they are the essence of creating peace in the world.

PART 6

Let Spirit Enter

```
I'VE GONE TO
FIND MYSELF
IF I GET
BACK BEFORE
I RETURN
KEEP ME HERE!
```

Opening Space

*Our homes are mirrors of ourselves. They reflect our interests, our
beliefs, our hesitations, our spirit and our passion. They tell a story
about how we feel about ourselves and the world around us.*

*A home is more than a place to lay your head and seek comfort from
the elements. It is a place where you can interface with the universe. It is
a crossing point in time and space that can attract energy and repel energy.*
Denise Linn, *Sacred Space*

A few years ago, I visited the home of a friend. This friend lives quite a distance from me, so our visits to one another's homes are infrequent. As I pulled
in the driveway, I was taken by the setting: a spacious, colonial style house,

surrounded by beautiful trees in a neighborhood of similarly appointed homes. I looked forward to the end of my journey and to relaxing with her.

When I entered the home, however, I was surprised by what I found. Every surface of every table, counter and shelf was laden with books, paper, things of all descriptions. Boxes were pouring out of cupboards, the doors no longer able to close. The clutter extended throughout the house. I had never experienced such an accumulation of stuff. It absolutely took my breath away.

Of course, my friend is not an exception; we all accumulate clutter—collections of this and that, files and books that haven't been opened or read for a decade, clothes that no longer fit us, or furniture that has long outlived it usefulness. It gathers, until one day we look around us and realize that we are lost in all the clutter—so lost, in fact, that we can no longer even find ourselves. We need to ask how our physical environment speaks to the life we are leading. Is the chaos around us an indication of our own inner chaos, a lack of clarity regarding the direction we want our lives to take? Are we moving through life like a whirling dervish, a little here and a little there, too much energy expended in too many different directions?

In his facilitation work with different communities, Harrison Owen says simply, "open space and spirit will enter." I have decided to open my space, to begin the process of de-cluttering my life on the physical plane, hoping that this will allow my spirit to enter, that once again I will find myself. I want to keep those things that have special meaning to me and which are necessary. I want to rid myself of the abundance of superfluous things in my life—stuff that simply takes up space, that has been sitting there unused for too long. As I begin the process, I have decided to use the following criteria as a screening tool:

- What adds meaning to my life? What is irrelevant?
- What makes me feel full? What drains me?
- What gives me a sense of comfort? What weights me down?
- What enhances the flow of energy? What blocks it?

Our physical environments need to be a sanctuary, a place where we can feel safe and at home with ourselves. In his book *Reclaiming Higher Ground*, Lance Secretan also suggests we need environments which are a "soulspace," a place of beauty, color and peace. Clutter is a distraction. Simplicity opens the space. So I offer you the following challenge: What actions will you take to de-clutter your life and open the space around you? Start with something simple and tangible. For example, take a look around your house. Check countertops, bookcases, cupboards, your office, the bedside table and bureau, your purse and your briefcase. How much stuff has accumulated and what can be discarded? How much of this stuff is important or holds any meaning to you? Are you feeling "stuffed-up"?

Next, check the closet. What fits you? What buttons up and what doesn't? What do you love to wear? What do you wear simply because it's there? What have you avoided wearing for the last few months? What can be given away?

Finally, create a Spiritual Space for yourself. Choose a place in your home and turn it into a sacred space, a place that is yours and yours alone, that centers you and continues to remind you of simplicity. This may be a shelf in a bookcase, your desk or a table in a quiet corner. Clear everything from the surface. Now carefully choose a few items for this space: things that inspire you and help you to breathe, things that remind you of your sense of purpose or your values. These might include a feather or special stone, a set of inspirational cards, a photo or something given to you by a special friend, or simply nothing, an empty space designed to receive that which has not yet been given to you. Remember, less is more; don't add much. Use this space to quiet yourself, to clear the energy field around you. Sit close by and meditate. Make sure your Spiritual Space represents what you seek within.

Travelogue

Journaling Questions

Look around you. What three things can you do to:

- reduce clutter?
- simplify your life?

The De-clutter Challenge:

- Clear 10 items of clothing from your closet.
- De-clutter your workspace—desk, filing cabinets, book shelves, briefcase.
- Create your Spiritual Space, that special corner which is just for you.

Travel Tip

Sometimes we travel through life with too much baggage—physical, emotional and spiritual. It is time to reduce the load. Start by limiting what you carry; de-clutter your home, your office, your mind. Allow the space to open. You will not only have better mileage, your windows will be clear and the direction ahead more visible.

Naming What We Want

[Vocation] comes from listening. I must listen to my life and try to
understand what it is truly about—quite apart from what
I would like it to be about—or my life will never represent anything
real in the world, no matter how earnest my intentions.
Parker J. Palmer, *Let Your Life Speak*

Have you ever renovated your home? As 2002 ended, we found ourselves in the middle of a small renovation project. I was amazed that a simple concept in my head became so complicated in reality. Take down a wall, turn what was a closet into a sitting area, put down a new floor, add a light fixture, and bingo, done. I thought I had been clear about what I wanted, but five weeks later the dust was still there, the construction uncompleted, and I was growing impatient.

Everyday, I questioned the contractor, seeking clarity about what he was doing and when the project would be completed; everyday, I got vague non-committal responses. I am thinking that the next time I do this, I will need to ask many more questions and be much more specific about what it is I actually want.

So here I was—that simple idea had taken on its own life. My desire to open the closet space and shift the energy and add light upstairs took on all the twists and turns that most renovation work requires. Another apt metaphor for life, I thought… All those things I have been trying to simplify, the spaces within me that I have been trying to open up, have also have been bogged down by unseen demons, unanticipated complications and unexpected curves in the journey. I need to shed the unwanted layers, to open myself up spiritually and to know what it is I want in this life.

Welcome to the new WORK ZONE! Start by thinking of yourself as a butterfly, a larva about to be transformed into a creature of great beauty. The final phase of our metamorphosis is to shed the cocoon, and in the shedding we show to the world all the beauty that has been just below our surface. Spiritual de-cluttering begins with renovation, the shedding of the many skins we have accumulated over our lifetime, skins that consist of the expectations of others, the influence of our education and culture, and the many experiences of a lifetime.

It is important to pause and examine both our own lives and the lives of others around us. What do we see? Notice the accumulation of spiritual clutter. These are the things we are told we must do, the rules by which we must play. These are the expectations attached to the various roles we occupy as wife/husband, mother/father, son/daughter, friend or colleague. We rarely ask how we sustain and nurture these relationships or how they do the same for us. We are schooled, ruled, educated and cultured, adding more layers to our cocoon. We are frequently told what is an acceptable career or lifestyle choice, what position we should occupy in a family or within the workplace, and what direction others expect our life to take. But what is it we really want for ourselves? When I ask others what they want, frequently they can't answer. Try it yourself, "I want…"

The fact is, what we want often eludes us, for to become clear we must allow the layers of clutter, the "must do"s , the "should do"s and the "have to do"s, to drop away. As we divest ourselves of the layers, we begin to see a glimpse of the light, our light, buried deep inside us. This is the real work—the work of coming home, finding out who we really are and what we want for ourselves.

Begin by asking yourself:

- What expectations are being downloaded onto me—by my family, parents, colleagues, boss and friends?
- Are these expectations about my needs or their needs?
- Is this what I want?
- What do I want to start saying "NO" to? What do I want to say "YES" to?
- What is it I need to choose for myself to sustain me spiritually and emotionally?
- What is it I want to do and am willing to commit to?

- What choices will be in my best interest in living this life?

As we become clearer about what it is we want, we establish a set of boundaries that we can use to guide our life path and make the critical decisions that will change the course of our life.

Knowing what we want is not always easy. The future we want to claim for ourselves, the person we wish to grow into, is often a blurry target. But consider this: When what we want is unclear, describing how we will achieve it is impossible. In the end, we may look back and find a life unlived. So, **what is it you want for you?**

Travelogue

Sit down with a learning partner, someone you trust and who you know will challenge you lovingly. Choose a quiet place away from disruptions or interruptions. Facing each other, have your partner ask you, "Who are you?" Allow your learning partner to record your answers. Repeat the question, "Who are you?" over and over until you have filled an entire loose-leaf page. Do not judge your answers; simply allow the answers that pop into your head to emerge. There is no right or wrong.

Now repeat the same process responding to the question, "What do you want?" Again, have your partner ask you the question over and over. Allow your answers to emerge free of judgment. Fill a second page.

Finally, return to the question, "Who are you?" and alternate with "What do you want?" Fill a third page. Once you feel that you have emptied yourself of answers, switch roles.

Once both partners have completed this phase, review your lists. Highlight surprises, "aha" moments, or answers you may wish to discuss with your partner.

This is an exercise you may wish to repeat. Each time you do it, new levels of clarity emerge in response to, "What do I want?" Working with a learning partner is advisable. Sometimes the other person will hear things that you do not. Question and challenge one another to be as clear and concrete as possible.

Journaling Questions

- What do I want? What vision do I have for myself in the future? What is my future desired reality?
- What exactly will success look like, and feel like, when I get there?
- What makes this vision important to me?
- What will achieving this vision enable me to do or be?
- How does my future desired reality serve humanity?

Examine what has been living in your heart; what makes you feel inspired, what stirs your soul and spirit, what defines who you are? Record what it is you wish to become, rather than what it is you want to achieve. Commitment comes from the writing. Be as specific as possible.

Travel Tip

When we begin a vacation, it is important to define what experience we want to have. Do we want adventure, relaxation or challenge? In terms of planning the trip, knowing what we want establishes the coordinates—the places we will visit and what we wish to do in each location. Applying the same strategy to the journey of life means that we can live the life we choose if we are clear about what we want. This will determine which roads we take, which direction we follow, and when we need to speed up or linger. Get out the map for your life and enjoy the journey.

Dive In

The farther we go on the inside, the farther our impact is on the outside.
John Demartini, *The Breakthrough Experience*

In the last chapter, we asked the question **what is it that you want for you?** Clarity—describing your own unique personal vision—is the first significant step in manifesting the life you wish to live. You now have a sense of your future desired reality; however, the process does not end here.

Now it is time to dive in. By naming what it is that you want, you have painted a new landscape for yourself—the place where you want to reside, the person you want to become. Now it is time to fill in the details, check the road ahead, and ultimately make a commitment to what you are willing to do to move forward.

This phase of our process involves stepping back and assessing our current situation; that is, where am I now relative to what I want, what I wish to become? What is the distance, the GAP, between our vision for ourselves and who we are now? An assessment of the GAP helps us to plan the steps we will need to take to move forward. Sometimes the GAP we see is large, other times it is only a few short steps away. Start with the following questions:

- What is my current reality, my current situation?
- What is the distance between the future I desire and where I am today?
- On the scale of 1 to 10, how close am I to my future desired reality?

Once we have completed our GAP analysis, the next step is to evaluate the opportunities and obstacles we anticipate on our path. Beginning with the opportunities, we want to assess what relationships and support systems we currently have in place to nurture us. Next assess what new possibilities exist for growth. Start by asking yourself:

- What support systems do I already have?
- What new pathways, possibilities, are open to me?
- What new learning would I like to engage in?
- What new strategies will I need to consider to move things forward?

The obstacles we anticipate may be perceived or real. They may be disguised opportunities or simply self-limiting thoughts. Ask yourself what you would need to change, move around or overcome to reframe this obstacle. Again, try to remain open and accepting to all possibilities. Ask:

- What do I believe is hindering or blocking me from moving forward?

- Are these obstacles real or perceived, self-imposed limitations or restrictions placed on me by others or by circumstances?
- Have I examined them from different angles?
- How can I turn these obstacles into opportunities?
- What strategies can I employ to challenge my beliefs/perceptions?

Our last step is where "the rubber hits the road." None of the previous steps will mean anything without commitment, a willingness to own our power and take control of our life. We need to ask ourselves, "What am I willing to do?" and define our Divine Action Plan—those steps that we will implement incrementally, one step and one day at a time. Some questions you might consider:

- What am I willing to commit to?
- What specific steps do I want to engage in (the HOW)?
- How can I use my core values and sense of purpose to guide my actions?
- What support/coaching will I need? From whom?
- What are my time frames?
- How will I measure success?

I have learned that defining my personal vision, assessing the current reality and identifying the opportunities and obstacles is easier when diving in, making the commitment to do it. You may find yourself hesitating to sign your Divine Action Plan, your contract with yourself. Without it, however, the process breaks down, and all your good intentions about redirecting your life may disappear. In the end we all need to just "do it"! What do you need to do?

Travelogue

The GAP

For this exercise, you will need the following materials:

- a large sheet of paper (flip-chart paper is best);
- an assortment of felt-tipped pens in different colors; and
- a large work surface.

Find a quiet place to work, free of interruptions. Fold your piece of paper in two. On the first half of your paper, you are going to draw what represents for you "your perfect day." I suggest you leave out sleep. Focus your attention on sketching images that represent your waking hours and how you would choose to live each day if the choice was completely yours. Try to draw rather than write. This opens you to your right brain and your creative mind. If drawing seems too difficult, you can also draw a large circle and cut this circle into slices, as if it were a pie, representing what percentage of each day you would like to devote to different activities. Allow yourself 15 to 20 minutes to complete your drawing.

Stop here before continuing, and complete your drawing.

After you have completed this part of the activity, turn your paper over. Do not refer back to your first drawing. Now, repeating the same process, draw your "real day," a day in your life as you are currently living. Sketch, don't write or use the pie format if this is what you did previously. Allow yourself another 15-20 minutes for this step.

Once you have completed the second drawing, open your paper up, and compare the two drawings you have completed—your ideal day versus your real day.

Note what the significant differences are. This allows you to further clarify your future desired reality and compare it to your current reality. What is the GAP between the two drawings? What small steps could you take to begin to move toward your ideal or perfect day?

Remember, success rests on identifying the steps you can commit to. If you make individual steps too long, you will tire, perhaps even give up. Go for "chewable chunks of doable bits"!

Journaling Question

- If you could do anything you wished, without fear of failure, what would that be? Dream big and be bold.

Travel Tip

Planning the trip is only the first phase of any journey. Then we need to contact the CAA, acquire the maps, apply for our vacation time and book the accommodation. When the day arrives, we get in the driver's seat, and the real part of our journey begins. We have finally put our planning into action. The degree of planning is always an individual choice, but don't be disappointed. The journey only becomes real when we place one foot in front of the other, when we start clocking those kilometers on the odometer.

Our One True Authentic Swing

*My object in living is to unite my avocation and
my vocation as my eyes make one in sight.*
Robert Frost, *The Poetry of Robert Frost*

In the movie *The Legend of Bagger Vance*, Will Smith, playing the lead role as a caddy Bagger Vance, speaks to his young protege explaining that each of us have "one true authentic swing":

Inside each and every one of us is one true authentic swing, something we was born with, something that is ours and ours alone, something that can't be taught to you or learned, something to be remembered. Over time the world can rob us of that swing, it gets buried inside all our woulda's and coulda's and shoulda's. Some folk even forget what their swing was like.

Ever since I was a child, I have known that I was a teacher. Yet when the time came to make a decision to go on to university, I enrolled in physical therapy studies at McGill University. As a profession, physical therapy offered me some opportunities to teach, but a large part of the job was using various therapeutic modalities, assessing physical ailments and devising the appropriate treatment strategies. For the most part, I experienced it much like a garage—a human body shop.

The machines we used helped us manage the professional distance we were told we were to keep between ourselves and our patients. But the machines and this professional distance did not satisfy my need to get to know people or to interact with them in a way that helped them to learn how to heal their own bodies. I became increasingly disenchanted. The search for identifying my "one true authentic swing" began in earnest.

Despite what many would experience as a career-limiting choice, I was fortunate. I tried to focus on what I had rather than what I did not have. Physical therapy studies gave me a scientific discipline, an ability to assess and evaluate and to transform my findings into a plan. This has served me well both personally and professionally. I had many mentors who encouraged me to think outside the box, to see the range of options available to me that would serve my sense of purpose. As a result, in 1987, I began my Master's degree in educational psychology, a gift that to this day I am extraordinarily grateful for. This was a significant first step in becoming the teacher I dreamed of being.

As I look back over my 30-year career, I realize now that whether I was interacting with patients, working for the MS Society of Canada, running a rehabilitation department or teaching a course, I have always, in that authentic place, been a teacher, coach and midwife, helping others to birth their own knowledge. It has been my passion and my purpose throughout my life, regardless of what I was doing at the time. And although I have on many occasions strayed from this path, in search of knowledge, opportunity or simply something more, I have always returned.

What is your one true authentic swing—that deep sense of purpose buried within you that is your connection to your divine self? What is the question that has always been in the back of your mind to which you feel you need to respond? Think back to your childhood. What do you remember wanting to do when you grew up? Was this simply a "flavor of the month" phenomenon, or was it something that has lingered and which emerges in the quiet hours? When you look inside and take time to see yourself, what is that hole, that deep desire, which remains unfilled? What have you always known about yourself in terms of your purpose, your calling? What makes you feel the most passionate and connected with your spirit? What would be your perfect day?

Identifying our authentic swing is perhaps the most important work of all. I encourage you to take the time to be quiet, to remember what, throughout your lifetime, has been truly meaningful. Think about those times when you have made a difference for another person or have been of service to a specific cause. What information can you glean from these occasions and what do they tell you about your sense of purpose? What have been your great achievements? What were you doing when you felt complete, in body, mind and spirit? Take time to record responses to these questions and to connect the dots. Notice what themes begin to emerge. Let the themes inform you about your one true authentic swing.

Travelogue

My Life Map

In his book *Callings*, Gregg Levoy says we can "use art to bring us in line with our callings." Drawing, he maintains, allows us to "engage in the process of self-discovery that is essential to the discernment of a calling." Some refer to this as visual journaling. Take time to draw your life map and see what discoveries you make.

You will need the following materials:

- a large sheet of paper (flip-chart paper is best);
- an assortment of felt-tipped pens in different colors; and
- a large work surface.

This is a time to be reflective and to review your life to date. In recording your life path, you may wish to use one or more of the following guidelines as a way of capturing the highlights:

- What were the major crossroads—points in the road where you had to make a significant decision that changed the course of your life?

- What external events changed your life (marriage, births, deaths, illness…)?
- What side roads were attractive but which you steered away from?
- What dead ends did you experience?
- What were the significant *road*SIGNS along the way?
- What were the highlights of the journey—the great "aha"! moments?
- What were the swamps, deserts or places where your vehicle broke down?
- When was it difficult to keep going—the steep grades, mountains to climb?
- When faced with change, how did you respond?
- What were you immersed in when you felt most connected to your purpose?
- What were your great achievements along the way?

Now take your paper and pens and begin to draw your life path, highlighting what has been. Be as elaborate as you wish. Use images and words to describe your experiences. Take your time. This is your opportunity to reflect back on a lifetime. This is your opportunity to connect all the exercises and reflections from previous chapters.

Once you have created your life map, share it with someone. In your discussions you may wish to focus on the following:

- What were the times when you:
  – learned the most?

- felt in top form, on top of the world?
- served yourself or others well?
- felt most competent and connected?
- What information does this give you about your calling, your one true authentic swing?

Journaling Questions
- What, from your earliest memory, did you want to be/become?
- How does this measure up to who you are now, what your are doing, and how you are living?

Travel Tip

We have arrived at a fork in the road. One direction is obviously less traveled, yet it pulls us and cries out to feel the weight of our footsteps. We feel compelled to turn in this direction yet we make another choice, the well-traveled route. It looks safe and was chosen by many who went before us. Choices on the journey of life are not always easy. Our head too often overrides our heart. It is time to start listening to our own internal rhythm, the choices that ring out as being our one true authentic swing.

EPILOGUE

Travel Tips

Our travels have come to an end, for now. We see on the horizon the possibility of a new life, of living more authentically.

It is time to show up and be more present in our life, to start paying attention to the *road*SIGNS, those **Significant Insightful "Gold Nuggets"** that inform our **Soul and Spirit.** These are the daily synchronicities that breathe life into our search for our Authentic Self.

Whatever your choices, from this point forward, choose to love, honor and cherish yourself. Be true to who you are by respecting your core values and living intentionally. Identify your one true authentic swing. Make a commitment to yourself and sign your Divine Action Plan. Inhabit your days fully and enthusiastically. Embrace your life.

I wish you love, light and peace for the journey. These are your Travel Tips for Authentic Living:

1. Along most major highways, we see signs posted for REST AREA, an opportunity to pull out of the traffic, get out of the car, take care of our biological needs and stretch those cramped legs. When we are caught up in the busyness of our day-to-day routine, involving work and numerous

other "doings," we also need to stop and rest; we need time to work out the spiritual cramps, the accumulation of doing in lieu of being. Make a commitment to begin scheduling a minimum of 10 minutes each day to subside—your time for reflection, quiet and breathing. This may be the most important 10 minutes of every day.

2. It's time for a tune-up, time to check your battery, your oil and your fuel gauge to ensure that you are both connected to your battery *and* running on a full tank. Like our vehicle, we need to check in with our power source. Occasionally we must yield as we merge into the busyness of life, but if all we do is yield, we will become lost in the traffic. Knowing when to yield (and when not to) is important. On our journey of life, a connection to our personal battery, that deep sense of who we are and how we want to be of service, is what will help us go the distance.

3. Take time to STOP, pause, breathe and reflect. When something calls to you, like a child tugging at your sleeve, do not dismiss it. Allow yourself to leave the road you are currently on. Pull off on a side road or simply stop on the shoulder. You may miss something important if you fail to take the time to consider the SIGNS or the questions in your life and the message they contain. Stopping may result in a change in your life, a link to something from the past, or a lesson to be learned. STOP means STOP!

4. Turn the car radio up loud and sing along, or better still, sing in the shower as you start your day. Play road hockey with the kids next door.

Swap funny stories with a friend. Host a "Whine and Jeeze" party; let people get things off their chests and then have a good chuckle. Laughter, music and fun open our hearts and ease the difficulties we sometimes encounter on the journey. They lubricate our cylinders and give us better mileage. We all need to "lighten up" at times. It helps us live life enthusiastically.

5. Our core values are important *road*SIGNS for the journey of life. They tell us which direction is aligned with our purpose, inform us of the speed limit, and guide our decision making. Without them, we become disoriented, a traveler nonetheless, but one without a sense of direction. Take time to consider what your big rocks are, those core values that allow you to be true to the one person who is the most important person of all— yourself.

6. Ask yourself frequently, "Who am I?" and "What do I want?" Write down your answers. Form specific intentions related to your responses so that you can manifest the life you want. Remember these rules: "If you cannot name it, you cannot have it" and "If you can not see it, you cannot be it." Knowing what you want sets the direction for your life.

7. Understand that you are free. Know that only YOU can choose the path YOU wish to follow. It is easy to blame others or circumstances for the things that happen in our life. We believe that others are determining the direction we are taking or placing the obstacles we cannot seem to sur-

mount. We invest energy into emotions such as anger, envy, why me? Unfortunately, blame only defers responsibility. We fail to see the *road*SIGNS and, subsequently, fail to learn the lessons we are being called to learn. When we understand that we are free to choose and to assume self-responsibility for our life journey, we release the negative energy that keeps us in low gear. It is time to examine where in our lives we are not taking responsibility and to understand the consequences. It is time to release anger and blame, and to accept that we are free to choose our own authentic path.

8. Make a commitment to rise each day, take flight and follow your own path. Acknowledge and celebrate your uniqueness, and have the courage to live your life as you choose. Embrace your sense of purpose, that sense of what is right buried deep within, and let this be your guide as you negotiate through the maze of highways and byways each day. Live a life of service, loving yourself first and letting this love spill out to others within your community. Take note of the SIGNS which inform you of your True North. When you are pulled off-course by events or people, do not loose heart. Pick yourself up, take a deep breath, and remind yourself where True North lies. Set your course again.

9. Make a choice to be "good tired." Find ways of being connected to your own sense of mastery, what you do well. See how what you do makes a difference for others. No matter what job you perform, understand that no job is too small if your intention is to do good. Be guided by your sense of

right and wrong, your ethical center and your BIG ROCKS. If your wheels are aligned, the going is smooth. You arrive tired but not exhausted.

10. Express gratitude often, for whatever crosses your path—a sunset, a butterfly, a rainbow, a "V" of geese taking flight at sunrise, a hug, a sincere expression of gratitude from another, a difficult lesson. When we express gratitude for something we cherish, we open ourselves to receive more.

11. On the journey of life, we need fuel to stoke our passion and keep our spirit strong. We have a choice to make every time we gas up: low- or high-octane. The high-octane choice reminds us of our uniqueness and the contribution we make each day. It keeps our spirit fueled for the duration of the journey and allows us to appreciate the scenery. Make sure to check the quality of fuel you are putting in your spiritual tank. Choose only from the highest quality energy source.

12. As we travel the highway of life, we are constantly faced with choices. If I take that road what will I miss? If I go the other direction, what will I gain or find? We can focus on the things we missed or focus on the things we find. We can focus on what we don't have or we can shift and focus on what we do have. An emphasis on gain, rather than loss, allows us to live abundantly.

13. The road is not always a smooth one. There are bumps; there are right turns, left turns and U-turns; there are yields, stops and dead ends. All of these

*road*SIGNS imply a change in direction or a change in speed. Take the time to understand what these signs mean before reaccelerating. Assess how a change in direction can open you to new possibilities. Become an explorer.

14. Every life journey will have some dead ends—times when we are forced to change direction or even retrace our steps. If we embrace the opportunity that comes with these endings, we have an opportunity to redirect our life in new ways and to re-evaluate how we wish to continue our travels. As we let go of our normal routes and habits, we open up the opportunity for exploring new terrain and seeing new sights. Both are the gateway to new learning and personal growth, and the possibility of living in a more authentic way.

15. Signals and signs are often confusing. The direction we need to take or the choice we need to make may not be clear. We worry about things outside our control, and our fuel gauge slides to empty. Refill your tank. Focus on the things you can do, can influence and can affect. Your mileage will improve and you will arrive at your destination feeling rested and fulfilled.

16. Choose your traveling companions well: those who nurture your spirit and honor your gifts, those who love you unconditionally, those who support *and* challenge you and those with whom you love to spend time. These are your rightful travel companions.

17. Share your stories with others as you travel. Take time to listen to the stories of your companions, as well. Buried in the text of any story lies great

wisdom and opportunities for learning and healing. Stories provide fuel for our sometimes-empty tank.

18. For nighttime travel, we turn on our headlights so that we can illuminate the road ahead. We need to do the same for our journey through life: turn the headlights on and illuminate ourselves. Take a look at the abundance that has been given to you—your talents, your great strengths and the integrity of who you are. Love, honor and cherish your only lifelong traveling companion, YOU.

19. Everyday we have a choice to make: to walk the path of love, light and peace or the path of fear, darkness and violence. As Robert Frost encouraged us, take the road less traveled—the path of love, light and peace. These three core values are the essential spark plugs of a powerful engine; they are the essence of creating peace in the world.

20. Sometimes we travel through life with too much baggage—physical, emotional and spiritual. It is time to reduce the load. Start by limiting what you carry, de-clutter your home, your office, your mind. Allow the space to open. You will not only have better mileage, your rear window will be clear and the direction ahead more visible.

21. When we begin a vacation, it is important to define what experience we want to have. Do we want adventure, relaxation or challenge? In terms of planning the trip, knowing what we want establishes the coordinates—the places we will visit and what we wish to do in each location. Applying the

same strategy to the journey of life means that we can live the life we choose if we are clear about what we want. This will determine which roads we take, which direction we follow, and when we need to speed up or linger. Get the map for your life out and enjoy the journey.

22. Planning the trip is only the first phase of any journey. Then we need to contact the CAA, acquire the maps, apply for our vacation time and book the accommodation. When the day arrives, we get in the driver's seat, and the real part of our journey begins. We have finally put our planning into action. The degree of planning is always an individual choice, but don't be disappointed. The journey only becomes real when we begin to place one foot in front of the other, when we start clocking those kilometers on the odometer.

23. We have arrived at a fork in the road. One direction is obviously less traveled, yet it pulls us and cries out to feel the weight of our footsteps. We feel compelled to turn in this direction yet we make another choice, the well-traveled route. It looks safe and was chosen by many of those who went before us. Choices on the journey of life are not always easy. Our head too often overrides our heart. It is time to start listening to our own internal rhythm, the choices that ring out as being our one true authentic swing.

References

The following authors are referenced within the text of *road*SIGNS. I thank each of them for serving as *road*SIGNS for my journey.

Andrews, Lynn. *Tree of Dreams: The Alchemy of Power, Wisdom and Strength.* Carlsbad, California: Hay House Inc., 2002.

Beattie, Melody. *Journey to the Heart: Daily Meditations on the Path to Freeing Your Soul.* San Francisco: Harper Collins, 1996.

Bloch, Deborah and Richmond, Lee J. *SoulWork: Finding the Work You Love, Loving the Work You Have.* Palo Alto, California: Davies-Black Publishing, 1998.

Ban Breathnach, Sara. *Simple Abundance: A Daybook of Comfort and Joy.* New York: Time Warner Books, 1998.

Bridges, William. *The Way of Transition: Embracing Life's Most Difficult Moments.* Cambridge, Mass.: Perseus Publishing, 2001.

Covey, Stephen. *Principle-Centered Leadership.* New York: Fireside Book, Simon and Schuster, 1990.

Covey, Stephen. *The Seven Habits of Highly Successful: Powerful Lessons in Personal Change.* New York: Fireside Book, Simon and Schuster, 1989.

Davis, Laura. *I Thought We'd Never Speak Again: The Road from Estrangement to Reconciliation.* New York: Harper Collins, 2002.

Demartini, John. *The Breakthrough Experience: A Revolutionary New Approach to Personal Transformation*, 2002. London: Hay House Inc., 2002.

Frankl, Viktor. *Man's Search for Meaning.* New York: Washington Square Press, 1985.

Frost, Robert. *The Poetry of Robert Frost.* New York: Holt, Rinehart, and Winston, 1969.

Gibran, Kahil. *The Prophet.* New York: Alfred A. Knopf, 1972.

Goldberg, Nathalie. *Writing Down the Bones: Freeing the Writer Within.* Boston and London: Shimbala, 1986.

Hendricks, Gay and Kathlyn. *Attracting Genuine Love.* www.hendricks.com, 2002.

Irvine, David. *Simple Living in a Complex World: Balancing Life's Achievements.* Calgary, Alberta: RedStone Publishing, 1997.

Jampolsky, Gerald. *Love is Letting Go of Fear.* Berkeley, California: Celestial Arts, 1979.

Jampolsky, Gerald. *Forgiveness: The Greatest Healer of All,* Hillsboro, Oregon: Beyond Words Publishing, 1999.

Levoy, Gregg. *Callings: Finding and Following an Authentic Life.* New York: Three Rivers Press, 1997.

Linn, Denise. *Sacred Space: Clearing and Enhancing the Energy of Your Home.* New York: Ballantine Wellspring, 1995.

Markova, Dawna. *I Will Not Die an Unlived Life: Reclaiming Purpose and Passion.* Berkeley, California: Conari Press, 2000.

Messer, Kerry. *My Wedding Vows.* Unpublished work used with permission of the author, 2002.

Myss, Caroline. *Sacred Contracts: Awakening Your Divine Potential.* New York: Harmony Books, 2001.

O'Donohue, John. *Anam Cara: A Book of Celtic Wisdom.* New York: Cliff St. Books, 1997.

Owen, Harrison. *Open Space Technology—A User's Guide.* San Francisco: Berrett-Koehler Publishers, Inc., 1997.

Palmer, Parker. *Let Your Life Speak: Listening for the Voice of Vocation.* San Francisco: Jossey-Bass Publishers, 2000.

Pressfield, Steven. *Legend of Bagger Vance.* New York: William Morrow and Company, 1995.

Ruiz, Don Miguel. *The Four Agreements.* San Rafael, California: Amber-Allen Publishing, 1997.

Ryce, Victoria. *By Me, About Me: Writing Your Life.* Vancouver: Raincoast Books, 1997.

Secretan, Lance. *Reclaiming Higher Ground: Creating Organizations that Inspire the Soul.* Toronto: Macmillan Canada, 1996.

Stepanek, Mattie. Cited in "What I Know for Sure," *O Magazine*, p. 189, Volume 3, Number 11, November 2002.

Walcott, Derek. "Sea Grapes" from *Collected Poems, 1948-1984*, 1988.

Walsch, Neale Donald. *Conversations with God: An Uncommon Dialogue, Book 1.* New York, G.P. Putnams Sons, 1996

Wilder, Barbara. *Money Is Love: Reconnecting to the Sacred Origins of Money.* Bolder, CO: Wild Ox Press, 1999.

Williamson, Marianne. *Return to Love.* New York: Harper Collins, 1996.

Winfrey, Oprah. Cited in "The Way of Truth," *O Magazine*, p.19, Volume 3, Number 1, January 2002.

Betty Healey, M.Ed.

Seeing the *road*SIGNS in her life has led Betty Healey to a greater understanding of her life purpose as a "guide on the side." As an author, personal discovery coach and engaging speaker, Betty is committed to serving others in their journey to reconnect with their purpose and passion. As the president of *people*HEALTH™ (www.peopleHEALTH.ca), an organization committed to "cultivating spirit and values in the workplace," Betty works within both the public and private sectors, supporting personal development (leadership), igniting team spirit and encouraging workplace renewal. Her work has taken her across Canada and to the United States and Scotland.

Betty also has a private coaching practice, Conrod-Jacques Consulting Inc., and offers a series of *Authentically*YOU™ retreats, which incorporate the lessons within *road*SIGNS.

**Betty is a proven workshop facilitator and keynote presenter.
To share Betty's message with your group or organization,
please contact Creative Bound Inc. at 1-800-287-8610
or visit our Web site at www.creativebound.com.**

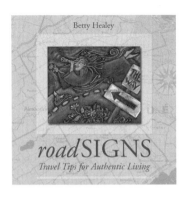

We hope you have enjoyed

*road*SIGNS

Travel Tips for Authentic Living

To order additional copies of
*road*SIGNS by Betty Healey,
please visit **www.peopleHEALTH.ca**
or call Creative Bound Inc. at **1-800-287-8610.**

Organizations, businesses and retailers—
ask about our wholesale discounts for
multiple-copy orders!